When God Leads And I Dare Follow

WHEN GOD
LEADS
And I
Dare Follow

BY CHRISTINA G. MIYANO

XULON PRESS

Xulon Press
2301 Lucien Way #415
Maitland, FL 32751
407.339.4217
www.xulonpress.com

Cover photo courtesy of Taka Miyano.

Printed in the United States of America.

ISBN-13: 9781545676783

Dedication

I dedicate this first and foremost to God. This is HIS design. Though seen through dimly-lit human and fickle eyes, I could not write what He did not purpose for me to do.

I also dedicate this to my husband, Takahito Miyano, to my children, Lin, Senoka and Masato, and to all our Gateway kids, from beginning to end, those who have stayed and those who have left.

Table of Contents

Foreword

*W*hen my uncle, who's the main pastor of my church, Shinshiro-church in Aichi Prefecture in Japan, shared with me about his visit to Gateway in Cambodia in 2013, it made me feel that I wanted to visit there so deeply. When I finally made my first trip to visit in 2014, the Gateway family became my precious family.

The moment of my first visit still stands out in my memory. There were more than 20 kids, ages around 5-15 years old. They were full of smiles and happiness. I could feel that love is always there. One of the impressive moments was when I saw how the Gateway family praised God together.

When it was Christina's turn to lead the worship, she was playing the guitar, singing worship songs in Khmer, and jumping and shouting with the kids like she was a girl! Christina was so full of joy and energy and sharing the love of God to kids and the place was filled with the Holy Spirit. For me, I felt that she is the coolest and a most wonderful woman who truly and sincerely loves God.

This book shows Christina's unshakeable belief, such as loving God first, being faithful and never doubting God. Through her words in this book, I have been so amazed to see how God guided her in His wondrous way. At the same time, I can't wait to see how God will continually bless and lead the Miyano family and

Gateway in His amazing way. I can guarantee that when you finish reading this book that you'll have a deep desire to serve the Lord in His special and specific way.

Aki Takimoto is a freelance florist who also serves at her Church's Ice Cream shop in Japan, which is used as a ministry to open doors for non-Christians to hear the gospel. She is also serving the music ministry (called Zawameki) in her church and she travels with her parents as they bring new songs of worship to all the churches all over the world to seek for a worldwide spiritual revival.

Acknowledgements

irst of all, I could not have found the time or space to write this if it weren't for my husband, Taka. You created space and pushed me out of the house for overnight writing retreats. I am so blessed that you would partner with me in looking after ALL our children and sacrificing your sanity and time for work so that I could have the ability to clear my head enough to get words down on paper.

I want to thank, also, my best friend, Karen Lehmann, who has been my bundle of joy, my confidant, my sister in Christ for the last 21 years and has helped me, encouraged me, and sustained me through my insane moments. To quote our favorite song, "you have blessed my life – more than you'll ever know."[1]

I thank Karen Lehmann, Areanias Mathis, Aki Takimoto, and Elizabeth Trotter, for your honest feedback on the words in these pages and for challenging me to write more about the hard parts than I was originally willing to do. You gave me courage to go deeper, and I am blessed for it.

Thank you to my parents. Your love and support have been a mainstay blessing in my life and I am truly grateful and blessed. I love you BEST!

---

[1] Watermark, "More Than You'll Ever Know," *All Things New*, Rocketown Records, 2003.

Preface
by Christina G Miyano

*W*hen I began thinking about writing, I was still unsure as to what I would write. I had dabbled in poetry and songs, but never anything as prolific as this. Yet, the desire was there. I just didn't know for what purpose or to what end.

As I continued to pray about what it was that I wanted to say, that I needed to say, I had to really search for the source of this desire. What was motivating me, compelling me, to write my story?

Having kept journals since 2000, I began retracing my recorded experiences that make up my own life. The undergirding and over-laying of my whole life is God. He is the One who is in control and who has given me all the experiences I have had and has enlight-ened my eyes with His truth to allow me to step ever forward as He calls me and I listen. I don't mean to say that I don't balk every now and then and that I don't have any regrets. I do. My life is riddled with the pinholes of selfishness and pride; of brokenness and pain.

But it is His light that continues to glow and to fill me. Time and time again, I see His hand held out to me, beckoning me closer to His embrace.

My hope is that whomever reads these words will not think about me, but to think about the One who leads me. I could not have had the courage in myself to go all the places He has led me to and through all by myself.

One other thing compels me: the message that we are the body of Christ and that we are to work together to edify other members of the body and to bring in new members. How can I edify the body of Christ if I cannot be authentic with the fact that it is only by God's grace being poured out on me and my life? He is my all. He is my everything. He is my "more than enough." We are never alone. We are made for community. God's community. And perhaps you too can find the peace I have as you continue the path set before you and you live the life God has called you to live – as *you*, for there is no other *you* in this world. You were made for a purpose – *HIS*.

Journal Entry: June 8, 2011:

Lord, help me to be whom You created me to be:

A woman full of

    longing for relationship,

        kindness,

            wisdom,

                insight,

                    purpose

– all components of extravagant love.

Chapter 1

From the Beginning

*E*veryone's journey starts from the beginning of life. Mine is no different.

I was born in 1979 to two loving parents and an older brother. At the time, my dad was stationed in New Orleans, Louisiana with the U.S. Coast Guard. Since we stayed there just over a year after I was born, my only connection is the information on my birth certificate and a few photos. My second autumn my dad was ordered to the Coast Guard Cutter SEDGE, an ice breaking buoy tender in Homer, Alaska, where he promptly left my mom, brother and me (ages three and a year and a half) to report aboard the ship in Hawaii, while the SEDGE was there for refresher training before sailing back to Alaska. Mom was left to work out transportation and supplies for the fast-approaching Alaskan winter since our car had been shipped to Anchorage but had not yet arrived.

I do not have a lot of clear memories from these first years in Alaska, but one thing I do remember is that sometimes my dad would be home in the evening but be gone by the time I got up in the morning. I would sneak out of my room quite often on the nights he was there to make sure he was still there, much to my parents' aggravation. We were there just shy of two years; sixteen months of which my Dad was underway on the ship.

The year I turned three, my dad was transferred to Anchorage, Alaska. This is where my early memories started to latch hold in my mind, and I recall the next six years of living there with great joy. We attended church quite regularly and formed lasting friendships with several families. In fact, from the time I was 5 or so, I spent my summers with another family that had two girls my age. During those summers, my parents would see me only when we would be at church together. I was in heaven living with my best friend and her siblings.

At a relatively early age, when relatives started visiting our "exotic" Alaskan home, I was introduced to certain games that later would be revealed as molestation. At the time, I didn't consider it as wrong as it was introduced by someone I loved and trusted. There were times when I would have the impression that there was something wrong in it, especially since we always "played" when we were supposed to be sleeping, and also because I was told to keep things secret from my parents. Our interactions with this relative were limited due to our distance geographically, but he was quite persuasive and an enthusiastic "teacher" that left a legacy that stayed with me into middle school years when I finally had the courage to say, "No more."

The summer I turned seven I remember watching my brother, my best friend and her sister all go forward in church to make a profession of faith and to be baptized. I knew that Jesus was in my heart, but I also wanted to be baptized. So, one Sunday, I finally had the courage to go down to the front and when the pastor asked me what I wanted, I told him that I wanted to be baptized. At the time, I didn't quite understand why the pastor sent me back to my pew without pronouncing my decision to the congregation as I had seen him do with everyone else. He told me that he didn't think that I understood what it was that I was asking for. I was embarrassed and ashamed that I somehow didn't meet the criteria needed to be baptized. Were these secret games the cause? My dad had already explained that I didn't need to pray for Jesus to come into my heart every day—that if I believed that He was my Savior, then Jesus was already in my heart and would never leave. I didn't know I needed to have the 'right' request when I went to the front of the church to ask to be baptized. After several months of being questioned and observed by the pastor, and with the added endorsement of my Sunday school teacher, I was finally baptized.

Growing up in Alaska left a bit of "wildness" in my heart. That, in conjunction with this twisted secret of sexual abuse, left me with inner chaos. Outward appearance may have shown me as one who "had it all together," but inside I was in turmoil. This is one of the side effects that these molesting games had on me. I became a hollow shell, wearing a mask. In a way I was a fake. I did what I was told; I was the epitome of a "goody two-shoes," but inside I was rebelling and sabotaging my relationships with others because, in my twisted understanding of relationships, anyone could turn into a monster and no one was "safe." I also struggled with the dichotomy of being *good enough* and had a great fear of rejection from anyone who might stumble upon this terrible and dark secret I was harboring. I presented myself as someone who is not easily rattled and could take any challenge that was dished out. I was a tomboy who could do nearly as well as the other boys at their climbing and sporting antics.

I held most people at arm's length from my heart. I was afraid of what people would think of me and my family if they knew about the twisted relationship that was within our walls. Though I was outwardly very friendly and outgoing, most people could not pinpoint who I truly was for they only had the portrayal of what I permitted to be known. In fact, it wasn't until my University years that I finally began to let others see past the mask to the true murkiness I was trying hard to weather and overcome, and even then only to a very select few. However, even with this sharing, I was still very self-conscious and only allowed each person a piece—never the same piece, and never the whole.

The summer I turned nine, my dad received a very big promotion and we moved from everything familiar and known, to the unknown and rather rough and brutal city of Philadelphia, Pennsylvania. This was a place where young people were getting murdered for leather jackets and expensive sneakers. In fact, a schoolmate of mine was killed during a drug-drop our first year living there. He was nine. I was especially disenchanted with the school since the system was behind academically where I was in Alaska and most of my first year was spent in review. My brother and I were kept busy, though, joining Boy Scouts and Girl Scouts and trying out for school sports. We lived outdoors after school until dinner time. But I never found another connection for a friend while there. In the military world, families come and go quite frequently. A usual tour of duty is three years. Most families move on when the tour is over; on to the next assignment. It is difficult for the children to make lasting connections, either with other military kids or with kids at school. This sense of impending separation left me with little desire to "go deep" with any friendship.

After the first summer in Philadelphia proved to have limited opportunities for us kids to keep busy, my mom decided that we should drive the nearly 5,000 miles to visit family and friends in Alaska. By then my aunt and grandmother had moved up there from Georgia. My aunt had already remarried, and my Grandmother had met her future husband who was then grieving the recent loss of his first wife to cancer.

We drove up in the family minivan with the middle bench taken out. With only my mom as the driver, my brother and I would take turns riding shotgun and playing navigator with the huge road atlas. We also had our two dogs with us. I remember our first day we were supposed to stop somewhere in Ohio. When tornado warnings were being issued on the radio, Mom told us that we were *not* going to stop in Ohio. Since it was my turn to navigate, and on the big map and the distance to Chicago was less than an inch, I asked Mom if we could make it to Chicago. We forgot about the state of Indiana in between!

So…a 5,000-mile drive took us six full days, not counting some layover stops along the way. It was a summer of fishing and visiting. It was also another encounter with my "game master" relative, but it was this visit that the molesting was brought to light to the adults, admittedly, by me when I refused to stay with the kids and was asked why. What a mess it turned out to be…though, looking back, as a girl of eleven, I was quite sheltered from just how severe it was for my cousin and their family. We were taken to a counselor and interviewed individually. Aside from this, I did not know what storm was brewing beyond the recounting of events. It was never spoken of again in front of me. I hadn't intended for the great "rift" to happen in their family. It caused so much anger and turmoil. I was just relieved that it was out in the open and thought that it would put an end to the abuse. That was also the last summer I wore the ever-popular miniskirts. To me, miniskirts meant inviting boys to touch me. I did not want to be touched.

When we returned to our home in Philadelphia, the abuse continued. At times I acquiesced willingly; other times I was reluctant, but often gave in to the pressure. The times I gave in gave me a mindset that what I wanted didn't matter – that for some reason, I was to do as I was asked or told to do regardless of how I felt. After that summer in Alaska, I began stealing. In all likelihood, I was trying to do as my brother did, but without getting caught. Some of his antics were cool, so I would try to mimic on some level to see what it felt like to get away with naughtiness.

My life in Philadelphia seems like a suppressed memory; and we lived there *four years*! During the last months of our life in Philadelphia I was caught stealing and had to take a ride in the back of the Military Police vehicle. I had been developing my stealing habit little-by-little, but that time I had gone beyond what I had ever done before...and was caught. I remember the humiliation of being followed out of the store and accosted by the manager in front of my neighbors. I also recall the devastation I felt as soon as I saw my mom's face. Oh, the shame I felt. Thankfully, this was enough to cure me of that habit. In the end, after that last time and getting caught, I was never the same. I had lost the urge. The price was not worth it to me in the end.

That same summer, I turned thirteen, and I was overjoyed with the news that our family would be moving to Alaska again. I was so relieved. I was ready for my life to "return to normal"-where I wouldn't stick out like a sore thumb with a strange accent and weird ideas of adventures. We moved to Kodiak, the biggest island in Alaska. Soon after we got there, I finally had the courage and strength to stop the molesting completely. Though this relieved the inner pressure and weight of guilt over my participation, I was not absolved of my conscious guilt over the years that it was present. Little did I understand it at the time, but the years of abuse would reverberate on the walls of my heart and corrupt many relationships before I was confronted with the façade I had made and the walls came crashing down while in University.

Our stay in Kodiak was a time of blossoming for me. It still took me a couple years to really feel comfortable in my own skin. Once I reached High School, I became known only as my popular brother's little sister. I wanted to be my own person. But I didn't know who that was. As I struggled with loneliness and some depression, I felt compelled to write to the relative who initially molested me and to apologize for any pain I had caused him and to let him know that I forgave him. Thankfully, he responded in favor of my request to rebuild our relationship. In the end, it lifted the burden I had been carrying to the point where I felt I was able to truly express myself. However, this was just one part of the healing process; a process that would take years and a very intense time of counseling while I was in university. Being new to this side of myself, it was a little slow in coming, like a turtle testing whether it was safe to come out...first one leg and then the other, then my nose flinching in and out. Still, with my inability to truly trust another with all of me, I left Kodiak without any lasting, deep friendships.

My High School years were busy and full. I was involved in the church youth group and traveling youth choir. I started going to the rifle/shooting range with my dad where I quickly climbed the ranks to establish myself as an expert in small-bore rifles at short range. I competed on the varsity swim team, tried out for wrestling (but quit after prelims since I was the only girl—and then as soon as I dropped it, 3 other girls joined). I joined the high school choir and drama club. I helped to start the high school air-rifle team and excelled in my studies, finishing in the top 10% of my class.

The summer I turned sixteen, my brother and I joined Life '95, which is a Christian Youth Conference. That year it was in Florida. It changed my life! God felt so powerful and so compelling for me. I had given my heart to Jesus when I was seven, but now I wanted nothing more than to serve Him with my life in some way – any way. After that conference, I joined the Youth Evangelism Explosion training through our church and learned how to share my faith with others.

My junior year my brother was away for his first year of University in another city. And though we had a rather unconventional relationship while children, by the time he had graduated High School, our relationship had deepened in love and companionship. He was my confidant as I waded through my own awkward adolescence. I was not to be lonely for long, however, because his room was taken over by a girl my age from Germany. Having her in our family was interesting. For one thing, I had never had a sister, and it was an adjustment as she learned to understand our "American English." She joined me on the swim team, and we helped her to learn how to drive our "jalopy" (a mix-matched truck with holes in the floorboards).

The summer I turned seventeen, I volunteered as a counsellor at a weeklong church camp for kids. At the end of the week, my mom broke the news that my uncle (my dad's baby brother) had committed suicide. I was devastated. Death had never been as real to me as then. Dad went to Texas to be with the family. My uncle and aunt had adopted four kids and they needed help and support from everyone available. I struggled a lot with depression over my uncle's death, though I didn't feel like I could openly share with anyone. I think I channeled my grief into busyness.

Heading into my senior year was exciting. My days were very busy. I had before and after school swim practices followed by a different activity every evening of the week. Then, after swim season was over, I got my first part-time job at a pizza and sandwich place on the Coast Guard base where we lived. It was a busy time, but I loved every minute of it.

Then, in the midst of all this activity, Dad received orders for another transfer. This time to St Louis, Missouri. He had to report for duty in November of my senior year. It was a tough decision to make, but we felt it best that Mom and I stay in Kodiak to let me finish High School with my classmates instead of uprooting in the middle of the school year. That same fall, my brother met and asked a girl to marry him while away at university. They came over for Christmas and were married in January. The whirlwind romance was due in part to the fact that she said she was pregnant. After they were married, she claimed to have had a miscarriage, a fact that was refuted by a doctor years later. It was following this that I wrote the following poem that I submitted to be published and it was chosen to be read in front of an audience.[2]

---

[2] Written and published under my maiden name: Christina G. Mathis

<u>Overcoming the Loss</u>[3]

My eyes are red from crying and here's the reason why —
Two people I loved fled this world without letting me say good-bye.
First was my uncle who in his garage he died
With the car running, leaving earth for a heavenly ride.
He loved us all but could not, with his debt, endure;
The welfare of his family, of that, he did ensure.
Miles away and having fun on my own,
Did I reside in a camp where the bright sun shown.
Sorrow filled everyone's heart but brought us all together
To realize that even without him our family was forever.
The other loss was as recent as two weeks past
When my unborn nephew from life lost his grasp.
My brother and sister-in-law were greatly saddened,
But because they are together, of that they are gladdened.
We all mourn this unfortunate loss,
But we are blessed by God who is our boss.
For He will never leave us no matter what occurs,
Because God has promised that His love will eternally endure.

By Spring Break of my senior year, the movers had come and packed up 90% of our belongings to gear up for our move to St. Louis. I had already applied to two different Universities and had decided on Southwest Missouri State University (SMSU) in Springfield, Missouri (now known as Missouri State University). I finished the school year without making many ripples on the outside world. My heart was simply waiting for the end of this chapter so that I could start over; start fresh: new place, new friends, and all of this done on my own. I was ready to test my wings of

---

[3] Fiorini, Laura, et al., eds. *With Flute and Drum and Pen.* The National Library of Poetry, 1997, p. 105.

9

independence. And so it was, on the day after I graduated, I said good-bye to what friends had come to see us off as we departed on the ferry. No tears fell. Only a wave and a smile as I turned to look ahead. I was not attached to anyone or anything emotionally. We visited with family and friends in Anchorage a few days before we hit the road to Missouri.

After a summer of helping my parents settle into their new home, I left to start university.

Chapter 2

University and Still Searching

irst of all, there is something to be said about my university life. I had chosen a university based more on location (it was near my grandparents) and tuition (since my Grandma had graduated from there, I was eligible for a scholarship). My major of choice was music. This seemed the logical approach, given my music background of singing in choirs since I was three and also spurred on by the Music Theory independent study I took my last semester of High school. Initially, I was advised to pursue the path of Music Education, but later found that it was not my passion. However, since I had already spent five semesters in the course, I changed the emphasis from a BS in Music Education to a BA in Music (voice) and added a minor in Creative Writing. By the end, I was more or less just interested in being finished, but I still had no distinct direction for my life, much less in using my degree for any marketable career. All was not in vain, however.

A few crazy accidents happened in that first year that really were blessings in disguise. First of all, I was assigned to live in a dorm that had been shut down for renovations. It was not even listed as an option for consideration in the Freshman Orientation package I received in the mail. It had no air conditioning, which meant that most people left their rooms open to the hallway, giving us a more communal experience. The only air conditioned room was the rec room where we congregated for pool, ping pong, and watching movies or playing video games. Coming from a smaller town, this sense of community and family really helped me to integrate in what I perceived as a safe environment. During the Freshmen orientation at the beginning of the year, I signed up for Bear Hair, which is basically the cheerleading "rejects" who wear really funky clothing, wigs, and face paint, and sit in a designated section to cheer on the Basketball teams. Out of this, I was introduced to Campus Crusade for Christ (hereafter referred to as Crusade) by one of the main leaders of the group.

Crusade held out a spiritual lifeline to me that not only gave me a faith community, but acted as a catalyst for growth in my relationship with Christ. I joined a Bible study that started as co-ed that changed to girls-only in later years. This group of young women came alongside each other as we stood together in facing of all the anxieties and triumphs one can encounter at university. Out of this group, I have been blessed to have a lifelong bosom friend who has prayed over me, for me, and with me ever since we first met. We have held each other up through relationship struggles with boyfriends and family.

I had a series of interesting roommates throughout my four years of on-campus life. One who was a diva, one who was kind of reclusive, another who was quite oblivious to boundaries when it came to borrowing-without-returning my things, and lastly, a rather studious freshman who put my academic pursuits to shame. I also had a series of boyfriends: two of which were kind of reckless and whirlwind romances, the first with whom I had my first kiss; the second with whom I first experienced being tipsy; the last being the "safety net" who was more best friend quality than romance. He was safe; he didn't demand anything from me, and I also knew that it wouldn't last. I believe that I did grow to like him very much, but he was heading in a different direction than I was, though most of the time, I did not have a clue as to where I was headed. In the end, I laid out the facts and we parted as a couple but maintained our friendship.

Throughout my University life on campus I was very much involved in and had great spiritual growth through the leadership and ministry of Crusade. Through Crusade, I had opportunities to do several short-term ministry trips and projects, including Yellowstone National Park (summer of '99-a summer with teaching emphasis on being a servant), Panama City Beach, Florida (Spring Break of '00), Hampton Beach, New Hampshire (summer of '00-a summer with teaching emphasis on being a teachable servant), and Chicago inner-city (Spring Break in '01). Through Crusade, my faith was challenged and solidified, and my burning desire and life focus was that Christ is my life and my life is for Christ.

Another aspect of this campus ministry was the retreats: one in the fall and one in winter. Our region's conference took place in Denver, Colorado. My second conference, January, 2000, brought to the surface some of the ugly truth behind the sexual abuse that I was subjected to when I was a child. I was in an emotional and spiritual upheaval. I believed that I had dealt with it and had moved on. Apparently, I had only scratched the surface. I bought *The Wounded Heart*[4] book and workbook at the conference and called a church near the University to find counseling to help me wade through the murky and frightening waters of recovery.

After the overwhelming emotional wave that hit during the conference and then initiating contact with a counselor, I was crawling through an emotional wasteland. I was numb. I didn't know how to function or how to start the healing process. I struggled greatly, having to really dig into the past and relive the memories in order

---

[4] Allender, Dan B., Ph.D. *The Wounded Heart: Hope for the Adult Victims of Childhood Sexual Abuse* NavPress, 1995.

to truly forgive everyone, including my parents (though they were oblivious, I harbored anger for their *not* knowing and/or protecting me). I was broken completely.

Toward the end of the semester, after all the minute details had been transcribed from my memory and submitted to my counselor, I just sat and wallowed in my self-deprecation. I was so filthy. I was so unlovable. I was so unworthy. It wasn't until nearly four months of counseling when I was journaling through the materials from the counselor, I came up short as I wrote that, although I had forgiven everyone, I could not forgive myself. That was the turning point in my recovery. As I laid it down at the altar, all the guilt and shame I felt, God's merciful hand touched and cleansed and released me from that burden.

However, though I received healing and felt free from a self-image and worth based on my past abuse, there would still be times when certain behaviors and sexual sin would re-enter my thoughts and affect my relationships with my husband and with God. I would still experience aftershocks of the abuse in my life. Anytime I battled with self-worth or value, the ugly truth of my past would rise up to jeer at me to feed the lies I would succumb to over and over again as I grappled with my identity as God's chosen daughter. And each time, as I would dig into the Scriptures of promise and of inheritance in Christ, His truth would pull me back from the brink of the abyss and I would weep tears of mourning and tears of joy in the revelation of His unceasing love for one such as me.

About that time, I first heard the song, "Grace" by Laura Story.[5] Her words were so profound to me that I copied them down in my journal and prayed them as my own:

---

[5] Laura Story, "Grace", Album *Silers Bald: Climbing*, 1997

Chorus:
I ask You: "How many times will You pick me up,
When I keep on letting You down?
And each time I will fall short of Your glory,
How far will forgiveness abound?"
And You answer: "My child, I love you.
And as long as you're seeking My face,
You'll walk in the power of My daily sufficient grace."...

While attending the Denver Christmas Conference for the third time, I was compelled to join the thousands of other University students to sign the Millennial Pledge: a promise to set aside one year of my life to full-time service, whether through Crusade or other entity. And so it was, in my last semester of University, I submitted my application to be considered to join Crusade on a STINT (Short-Term-Internship). Initially, I had submitted my application to join the Keynote Ministry, which is the traveling music ministry of Crusade. As graduation was fast approaching, I was starting to panic as my application to join the traveling music team had yet to receive a reply. My initial paperwork and phone interviews went well, but my auditions needed viewing.

Finally, as graduation loomed near, I was informed that my application was turned down for the music team, but I was asked if I would still consider doing a 1-year STINT elsewhere. Seeing nothing else on the horizon, I agreed. I explored my options: 1) going to Boston University and working with the Crusade staff to reach University students there (I had a connection with a staff couple from my time on project at Yellowstone) or 2) going overseas to someplace like Spain since I had studied 3 semesters of Spanish at University.

One particular journal entry captures some of the warring emotions I was going through during that time of indecision and unknown direction:

December 4, 2001:

I <u>do</u> struggle with jealousy of those who seem to
have their future plans all planned – as far as career
and/or marriage—and I really don't have a clue as
to what I will be doing if I don't go on STINT and/
or what I'll do after that year is up. I mean, I don't
have any real promising careers in my future with
my BA in music. It is a kite I let go of now, Lord,
and give to You. I ask that You take my future and
do with it as You will. Amen

I contacted my discipler (who had transferred to a new campus
by then) and talked things out with her by phone. At the time, there
was a new partnership for ministry in Central Asia, more specifically, in Kyzyl, Siberia. My discipler told me flat out that she didn't
believe that I would be challenged the way I would need to be
challenged in Spain; but rather, that she saw that I should consider
the new partnership in Siberia. Naturally, my first thoughts were:
"Siberia-?! Am I being punished or banished?" But, quite quickly,
the sense of adventure in me led me to contacting the current team
on that site and my heart began burning within me to set my focus
and prayers for Kyzyl.

I contemplated this new possibility as I headed to Denver for
what was to be my last Crusade conference. The day before the
conference was to start, I fell on the ski slope and tore my ACL.
So, I spent the rest of the conference in an immovable knee brace,
knowing that I would need to have surgery in the next few months
before my health coverage ran out. Knee injury or not, I was blessed
all the more with a confirmation of my accepting a placement with
any STINT team, regardless of where I would be placed.

As I spent the months following my surgery in February, I continued to maintain contact with the current team in Kyzyl while

going through the steps of physio therapy for my recovery. Though I had graduated in December, I still maintained my rental contract on a small duplex near campus, which enabled me to stay plugged in to campus ministry and my Bible study. Being surrounded with my spiritual support network was a blessing that continued to confirm my decision and I received much encouragement through the Crusade family.

"For My thoughts are not your thoughts,
Nor are your ways My ways," declares the LORD,
For as the heavens are higher than the earth,
So are My ways higher than your ways
And My thoughts than your thoughts."

-Isaiah 55:8-9

Chapter 3

Kyzyl, a Journey of Doubts, Depression and a Calling

*T*hat summer as I prepared to go to Kyzyl, I had many "nay-sayers" come into my life. Some were people whom I thought would have been more supportive, and some were from people I didn't even know. It was challenging. I was so blessed to have my best friend and others around me to support this decision and encourage me when I was faced with rash comments and unasked-for opinions. I had made a decision to follow God's leading and I didn't like, nor appreciate, people meddling with this decision. Even my mom was heard to say that my decision to go was just to hurt her. I know that she was speaking out of anxiety and fear for me being so far away, but it didn't lessen the sting of her remarks. I was able to talk to her about it and she eventually came around to seeing that I truly was acting in faith that this was what God was leading me to do.

It was a summer of spiritual growth and a lot of questioning. I had many people saying their own thoughts on what I should do with my life. But I also had some introspective thoughts as to the real reason for my going. I think there was a part of me that just wasn't ready for "real life" in the secular world. There were days that I was straggling through the wastelands of negativity and then moments of exhilarating peace, knowing that I was fulfilling my pledge to spend a year of my life in ministry.

In mid-August I flew out to Colorado to spend a few days with the team, getting to know them and praying over our location and our witness there. After a few days together orientating as a team, we boarded a plane to Budapest for an initiation conference of all STINTers going to spend the next nine-ten months in Eastern Europe. There we met the two people who would be in direct authority over us as mentors, though they lived in another Siberian city.

We finally landed in Kyzyl in mid-September – a relatively rural town on a flat plain surrounded by high rolling hills and a river. While we navigated the search for accommodations, we were given the chance to stay in a family's house while they were away on holiday. The interesting aspect was that due to there being no lock on the bathing room (toilets in Russia were in a separate room), I had the very embarrassing situation of opening the door on our team leader as he was about to step into the shower. This was *not* how I envisioned starting off on the right foot!

Thankfully, within a week we secured housing: with the three of us girls on the top floor flat and the two guys in the flat just below ours. Our team leader registered us at the University for Visa purposes. Three of our team actually signed up for classes to help integrate into the student population better, having a firmer grasp on the language while I found an outside language tutor – not only was I the youngest at twenty-three, I was the only one on my team who had never been to Russia and, therefore, was at a severe disadvantage with the language.

During the first week of explorations of our surroundings, one of the girls decided to challenge us all to a hike up a small mountain on the other side of the river. We had heard that the locals had dubbed it "Mt. Lenin," so that is what we called it throughout our stay. That initial climb dispelled the unmistakable truth that I was quite out of shape but did have the added bonus of allowing me to think more clearly about some aspects of my life.

> September 14, 2002 [after climbing a small mountain across the river in Kyzyl]
>
> I'm thinking now of how parallel today's climb is to our year here in Kyzyl. I'm sure we will each face our times when we want to just sit down and not even think of going on. Other times we may look ahead to being at home afterward and therefore miss some of the things You would like us to see and experience while on this journey. [Today] I got blisters and bug bites and sunburn. Oh that I would have marks from this year – visible passage with You as we walk daily together, Oh Lord!

I must say that I had some expectations going into our time in Kyzyl. I was star-struck to be in such a place and to try to reach students for Christ. However, I was not so prepared with the struggles that I would have within myself and my language abilities; or, I should say, *disabilities*.

I'll admit, there were things that I took for granted. And perhaps I was very naïve, but I was eager. I think that the greatest challenge for me was having to be so dependent on my teammates for language; especially in the beginning. I went from someone being able to interact verbally with anyone I encountered, to one who was observing the others while standing off to one side. It was definitely a new reality for me. Even so, I learned the value of being silent and observing. There was also the inner struggle of jealousy and even resentment of my teammates. I felt that I was more of a burden and at some points even withdrew myself from ministry outings because I just couldn't face my own failings (as I saw them) in communication.

During the course of the year, we decided as a team that each member would have scheduled personal retreats where we would all go someplace by ourselves to completely focus on God and His Word individually. For the three girls, two of us would go stay in separate hotel rooms while the third stayed at the flat. These retreats were so vital to keeping our spiritual, mental and emotional sanity. They created a lifeboat for me to swim to as I felt like I was nearly drowning in depression, competitiveness, and the misplaced expectations on myself and my team.

During our first retreat, I had the first inkling that God was calling me to more than STINT with my life. More specifically, for me to give my whole life into long-term overseas missions. With this rather clear image of God asking me to not just trust Him with the *bit* I had offered of myself in committing to this one year of STINT, I began considering what it would mean to give my life to full-time overseas ministry. Not long after this day with God, I was proffered the option of considering staying in Kyzyl another year with Crusade-an offer that, at the time, seemed to be a partial answer to the leading I was receiving.

Life in Kyzyl had a certain rhythm; one that was painless in some ways and rather painful in others, e.g.: monthly reports to Crusade due on gospel conversations and conversions; language deficiency on my part; near-constant migraines, etc. Our team struggled greatly over this. As it was a new partnership to a largely unreached people group, we felt that the rules were too rigid for us to even aspire to; yet, we still had to send in our reports. Even in some of the responses received from my sponsors to the newsletters I would send out, I felt like I was such a letdown to those who prayerfully and financially supported me to be there.

A couple times a month, my parents would call. After one such phone call, I had a particularly difficult time pondering my abilities as a missionary to strangers when it seemed that I had never really taken the time to make sure of the spiritual status of some of my most-beloved relatives. Once, my mother mentioned to me, after I had already fielded the option of possibly staying for another year overseas, that my grandpa was not very happy with the idea. He said something to the effect that he couldn't understand why I wanted to be so far from home. If he couldn't understand that I was acting on faith, and support my path, what did this say about his faith? What did this say about the fact that I had never had a spiritual conversation with him?

Accompanying this was a period of incessant migraines for more than 2 weeks and the niggling thoughts of doubt. It was difficult to be out of my element and unable to function in my normal capacity. But, allowing Satan to have this advantage over me handicapped my ability to be fully present in the ministry that we were there to do. There were times I was so confused and feeling so lost as to what all I was truly experiencing and feeling.

All this time, I was still contemplating what it was that God was calling me to do – whether to stay on another year or to venture into something different. I was also struggling with the fact that I had a deep desire to one day be married. It was a topic often written and prayed over in my journals. But my deepest desire always returned to want that which God had already appointed for me; even when I didn't understand:

December 9, 2002:

Lord, am I to join staff with Crusade?

Am I to do long-term missions overseas?

Am I to marry?

I cannot pretend that these things do not plague my mind and heart daily, dear Lord. You are with me, guiding and helping me each step of each day, yet, why do I fear so? If You are for me, who can be against me – yet still I tremble and worry. Am I to doubt You forever, dear, sweet Lord? ...

I want to serve You.

I want to travel

I want to fall in love and get married.

I want to be involved in some shape or form in a ministry – whether it be sending, serving and/or going myself.

I want to follow You, dear Lord.

Very early one morning a little over 3 months into our STINT, we were awakened by an incoming overseas call. Somehow, I was the one who managed to shake the cobwebs of sleep well enough to reach the phone first. However, I almost wished that I hadn't. It was my mom calling to tell me that my grandpa had had a massive heart attack and had passed away. I remember sinking to my knees and crying. I mourned the loss; I mourned the fact that I was so far away and that I would be unable to attend the funeral.

December 11, 2002:

Grandpa died today (December 10), dear Lord. He had a massive heart attack and fell. ... Be with me, dear Lord, as I go through all the grieving processes. Help me, Lord. This is going to be a hard time for all of us this Christmas.

One thing that pains me above all else is the fear that he did not know You. It breaks my heart! How foolish I was to not speak my heart to him about

Your saving grace! You know, Lord. I pray that You have him there with You, sweet Jesus.

Thank You so much for the last 5 years when Grandma and Grandpa were so close for me to build up our relationship. I will miss his quirky and fun nature. I will miss his phrases:

"Hello, love of my life"

"Hurry up and come out and see us!"

"When you comin' out?"

"Well, now, Honey…"

I will miss our early evening walks with Freckles and Saturday morning coffee time and going with him each week to get Grandma her rose.

"We're so glad you came to see us!"

I will miss watching as he searches every pocket for money and correct change whenever paying a bill.

"You'd better hold the wheel, it's liable to steer itself right over to WalMart."

"Well, there's a small matter of this list I'd be obliged if you would take care of…"

Lord today has been a LONG day. It has been an emotional roller coaster with the myriad of emotions I've been going through, dear Lord. At times, the thought leaves me completely and then Mom's voice, "We're down at the farm; Granddaddy passed away today." Oh, sweet Jesus! Thank You for the love and support You give me through my parents!

My Grandpa's death really shook me up. I didn't know what to do with all the thoughts raging inside of me. I didn't know how to behave, how to move forward. I was stuck. I didn't really understand just how deeply I was affected. I needed to move forward, but I was floundering. This is quite evident by the tirade of questions I had for God and myself in my journal a few days after I had heard of Grandpa's passing:

December 14, 2002:

Lord, where is my hiding place?

Where can I go when the world gets so cold?

Am I alone?

Am I ready and willing to suffer for You – that in my faith and joy in gladly suffering for Your cause that people will glorify <u>Your</u> name and not my own?

Am I willing to remain single?

Am I willing to go where You send me?

What am I doing here? Have I let Your light shine through me these last 3 months? Have I crippled Your work in and through me because I have not denied myself to You?

Do You call me here to work on me and not through me?

Did I not obey Your calling when I came here? When I broke up with [my boyfriend]?

Have I come here in vain? To escape the world in America? Or did I come because I felt You calling me to come?

Are You telling me to stay overseas?

Are You calling me into full-time missions/ministry?

What is holding me back?

Desire to marry and start a family

Desire to be near family (especially with the death of Grandpa still so fresh).

Why am I having such a hard time realizing the fullness of You and Your sufficient grace?

Why am I doubting that You will supply all my needs?

Why do I toil over giving up my life to You?

Why am I so weak?

Why do You bless me? I have done nothing to deserve them – I, even now, doubt.

Thank You for this refreshing release, dear Lord. I still need You, as I always have and always will, to reprimand, break and fill me each and every day. Bring me to this realization throughout every day so I may not be boastful in my own performance or myself. For it is no longer myself – but You, dear Lord.

Life in Kyzyl moved on. I couldn't just leave. Christmas was hard. It was my first ever to be without any family. But it was a blessed time as well. We spent some time away as a team where we took the opportunity to encourage one another and to clear up any misunderstandings. Through this, I was encouraged greatly and was helped to see what I couldn't see: to see how I really *was* a part of the team, regardless of how little I saw that I was contributing. God used my team members to show me that I was still necessary, and I was doing what He had called me to do.

After a mid-year conference to Estonia, a short vacation to Sweden, I headed back to Siberia with a clear head and heart. We had planned a winter retreat with many of the students we knew and arrived there just an hour or so before the first students arrived. I remembered that I was so exhausted that upon seeing our beloved students, I was on the verge of tears when I could hardly eek out an intelligible phrase in Russian! All was not in vain and I soon regained what little language I had before the break and was able to connect with some of our students on a deeper level.

During our second semester we girls began a holistic approach to fitness and wellness among the female student body with whom we had been building relationships. We were able to secure the use of a gymnasium and held hour-long exercise classes three days a week. At the end of each week, we invited small groups of the girls to our home for a healthy meal, with a lesson on physical health and bridging that topic to the matter of spiritual health. We wanted to girls to know that we were concerned with their whole health: physical and spiritual.

Though I took an active and supportive role in these outreaches, I was still suffering a deluge of conflicting desires and emotions. After all, I was, in all actuality, floundering with grief, depression, and my overwhelming struggle with what to do with my life after STINT.

February 24, 2003:

Oh Lord, what am I doing? I am cutting myself off here [missing ministry outings and events on

our regular schedule as well as some social out-
ings]? What am I doing? I am not being obedient
to Your call – I am merely surviving – not thriving
and I have become lazy and selfish with my time
and energy spent. <u>I am a fool</u>! Forgive me, Lord!
Lord, I have come to realize that I cannot say "with
<u>all</u> my heart" (Psalm 119:69b) I follow You or will,
dear Lord. I know that I sin and that I am weak.

Lord, You teach me, admonish, mold, guide and
encourage me so much by the Word of Your mouth
which I hear and I read. I am blessed because You
are my stronghold!

Through all these enclosing and depressing thoughts, I was
reminded of what God showed me in Isaiah 55 in October. It was
then (in October) that God told me that He didn't want just this bit
of my life – but that He wanted my whole life spent in His will –
as an overseas missionary. I had no idea where or even how – so I
wrote for advice from my parents and they pointed me in the direction of the Christian and Missionary Alliance (hereafter referred
to as the CMA).

While I searched the CMA website, I was also continually bom-
barded with emails from other Crusade staff and other STINTers to
persuade me to commit to another year in Russia, just not in Kyzyl.
To speak truthfully, all the pressure acted more as a repellant. No
matter how much of my spiritual formation was owed to the ministry and workers of Crusade, I could not see myself aligned to
them as a full-time worker/staff.

By mid-March, I filled out a self-assessment on the CMA website
to be considered as a possible missionary candidate. Re-STINTing,
was no longer contemplated. In a way, I was relieved. I wanted to
be home with my parents. I wanted to debrief and regroup in the
emotional safety I knew would be there.

In the end, we left on June 10th, parting with our friends and also parting with teammates. I made arrangements with a family friend and his family to pick me up from the airport so that I could surprise my parents. I showed up at their house and rousted them out of bed at a most unholy hour of 2am (I think) and we spent the next four or so hours unpacking and chatting away like crazy.

It was good to be home.

Chapter 4

Re-entry and Re-integration

Being home was a bittersweet reunion with my parents and my grandma. It was also a time of a spiritual decline after the initial euphoria of being reunited with family. When I came out of STINT, I was much more reserved and careful about my words and expressions. I was unsure how I would be accepted by my family, my friends. I grappled with how much I had changed spiritually and feeling the gap between my family and friends and life in general in the US. It was like I had been on "pause" while everyone else kept moving forward without me. I didn't fit. I felt displaced. I felt lost.

I remember the first few weeks that people would turn and ask me if I was okay. I was confused with their question and also confused with what they meant with *okay*. It came down, mostly, to the fact that I was not as chatty as I had been prior to STINT. I was much more reserved and quiet. It was difficult in some cases to even know what to contribute to particular conversations due to the fact that many times the conversations centered on things that had happened in my absence and I had no context.

Knowing that I needed to have some time away, my best friend and I planned a road trip to spend a week, just the two of us. We drove out to the East coast and stayed in New Jersey near Wildwood on the beach. It was a time of reconnecting and encouragement for us both. We talked about all the things that were left unsaid in our emails and my newsletters. We prayed together. We spoke truth over each other's lives and direction.

Within a few of weeks of my return, I was recruited on two fronts: 1- to join an inner-city ministry called World Impact, and 2- to help head up the youth group for my parents' rather small church for the summer. Initially, I was excited about the aspect of continuing ministry, but I was quickly disenchanted when it became quite obvious that I was to spend all of my time at World Impact doing office and clerical work with little or no interaction with other people in the community or in the office.

This placement left me a bit bitter, but also at a bit of a loss as to how to navigate what was needed of me versus what I wanted to do. I was also jealous of another summer volunteer who seemed much younger (19) and much less experienced, who was in the position that I coveted. She was living in the neighborhood where World Impact served and had a daily interaction with the community.

In the meantime, I contacted the CMA seminary in Canada and started the process of applying to their Master's program in Intercultural Ministries, setting a start date for the January, 2004, semester.

The fall of 2003, my Dad was retiring after serving 30 years in the Coast Guard and had accumulated nearly 3 months of paid leave. We decided to take the opportunity for a month-long drive up to Alaska. And since we would be driving past the seminary in Calgary, called Canadian Theological Seminary (I will hereafter refer to it as CTS—now known as Ambrose University), I decided to hand-deliver my application and tour the campus while we passed through.

During and after the trip, I fell into a state of disillusionment. I was sick of the state of pretense that I had fallen into. Yes, I was grateful for the time that I had spent in Kyzyl, grateful for the time of rich spiritual growth. But I was dissatisfied with life that was in the States and I felt an incredible lack of community. I struggled to care for the things that seemed to consume those around me. I had no base, no foundation, and no roots in America anymore. I had fallen into a trap of survival. People didn't know what to do with me and I didn't know how to share the deep burden for going overseas. And I suffered from niggling doubts: "Am I sure I heard God right?" I was impatient to start seminary, impatient to start living in the vision that God had given to me the year before. I wanted to be zealous, but instead I was mediocre and uncertain.

September 27, 2003:

> Lord, I must be frank with You. I have not been leading my life patterned after Your Word. I have been in limbo – waiting for the future to happen and I am not living to glorify Your Name in the here and now. ...Sure, I am looking forward to CTS and later to be a missionary, but right now, at this very moment, I am not zealous for You. I'm uncertain with pronouncing what I am pursuing to the world – why is that? Am I having doubts? Do I lack faith? Have I turned lukewarm? Oh consume me, Father! Encompass me – take me from here! Break me, Father! I know I need to walk by faith and not by sight – but my selfish, controlling nature wants the road signs and blatant clues to help me – to make things easy. I told [someone]...that the not knowing was the adventure in following the call and following You – so long as we are WILLING. I <u>am</u> willing!

Upon our return to Missouri, I called around to other churches in the area and found a Bible study group to join, seeing as I was

33

starving for some faith community that I wasn't receiving at my parents' small church. I was empty emotionally and spiritually. I believe that this is a common occurrence for those who experience great spiritual growth and fellowship and when it ends, it leaves a void that, if one is not careful, will swallow a person up, stagnating all pursuance of God.

I also applied for a part-time job working at a Christian bookstore. It was at these two places that I met some great encouragers to assuage my doubts of calling and for praying against my petty doubts. It was a season of being filled up and releasing all the negativity, the doubts and questions I was faced with. I do not believe I had experienced such a powerful whirlpool of emotions as at that time. The weekly Bible study and my co-workers held a lifeline to me, along with my family and my Bible study sister from University. At the same time, I still felt alienated by life around me.

November 7, 2003:

I am definitely lonely here, Lord. And I know that You sustain me and are sufficient and my portion forever – but I am lonely. Maybe it's because everything has slowed down that I am able to realize how empty my daily life is – when no one is around - ...I don't <u>DO</u> anything...Oh Lord, please fill me! [Song lyrics by Paul Colman] "Fill my cup to the top with running water, call me out and show me how..."[6]

---

[6] Paul Colman Trio, "Fill My Cup", Album *New Map Of The World*, 2002.

November 18, 2003:

I want to follow You, dear Lord. <u>Never</u> let me settle for <u>anything</u> short of what You have called me to do!

I want my life to be exemplified by the firm trust and faith that I have in You – but I am not there yet. I need breaking, dear Lord. I need and want brokenness. I realize that I am a gossip and that I am addicted to watching movies and television. I give all areas of my weaknesses and temptations over to You to make Your power perfect in my life for You are sufficient for me!

Life continued with the ebb and flow of seeking the Lord and grappling with the impatience of having to go through the process of learning and training before I could even be considered ready to go overseas. On January 1st, 2004, I landed in Calgary to begin my professional training at seminary.

Chapter 5

Seminary and a Burgeoning Romance

*L*eading up to my impending seminary arrival, I needed to work out the details of accommodations. After a brief search, I settled on sharing a house with a woman near my parents' age. Since I knew little of the geography of the city and its layout, I didn't realize that I would be living quite a way from the city center (where CTS was located in a high-rise office building). Regardless of how great the public transportation was, it still ostracized me from the community of most of the other seminary students.

During the first week at school I was re-introduced to a student, named Taka, whom I had met him briefly in September when I had dropped off my application. Taka was from Japan and was studying in the same degree program. He held weekly prayer-intensive meetings that I joined. We seemed to share the same restless spirit within us: that we were made for something more and we couldn't wait to get out and do it. In the meantime, we wanted to continue to feed our passion to follow God and wanted to spur others to do so as well. We were often in the same group of international students who would continue deep spiritual conversations at Tim Horton's, a popular coffee shop, or over some cheap and delicious Chinese food.

My classes were infused with so many new queries into my heart, my faith, and my shape as an instrument for God. I was asked about what I would do as a missionary. I had never thought about it before: the doing, the being. I had never thought much about a specialty or focus other than working with the people and bringing the gospel to them (such as we have done in the past in various ministry trips I had been invited on). This and other deep questions shook me and forced me to seek God for His answers for what He would use me for and how. He had made me. He was calling me. There must be a reason. There must be a how.

I found that I thrived at the seminary in all aspects of my life. I was spiritually charged with the weekly chapel meetings, the prayer meetings led by Taka, the content of the courses I was taking, and the close-knit community of students that I was welcomed into. I must say that I never truly studied academically before I went to Seminary. I was so enthralled with the materials and the deep burgeoning questions of faith and theology that I was faced with in class and in my deepening knowledge of Scripture.

I had truly found a wellspring and I was so thirsty. Often, I would arrive with the librarian at 7am and stay until after 10pm, followed by a trip to Tim Horton's or Second Cup (another coffee shop) with a small group of other studious students to continue conversations that only spurred on my spiritual craving for more and more. Indeed, I clung to these coffee-shop meetings until the last bus or train would leave the downtown area. With all this euphoria, there was coupled a sense of uneasiness and dissatisfaction. I wanted to *do* something with all that I was learning. I didn't want to contain it, and I struggled with finding an outlet for what wanted to overflow out of me.

At the end of that first month, I was invited with other international students for a day retreat at one of our professor's house. It was there that I laid out to God my desires for relationship before going on the mission field. There was an attraction for Taka that I couldn't shake. I had experienced attraction to other great men of faith, so I was not certain how to handle myself around him: was it just being enamored or was it something more?

The first weekend in February there was a retreat for all the seminary students and professors to simply get out of the city and spend time diving into God and to pour ourselves into our community, building lasting relationships and to spur each other on in our walks of faith and calling. The morning that we were to leave, though, I found Taka on the phone talking in Japanese. After he hung up, he told me that he had just found out that his grandpa had passed away. He seemed distant and I didn't really know how to talk to him then. However, knowing from my own experience of being away from family during a time similar to his, I wrote him a letter sharing scriptures that had comforted me while I was grieving the loss of my grandpa from overseas.

My letter seemed to open a portal for us to talk during the retreat. We spent a lot of our free time together, talking and taking walks in the winter wonderland around the retreat. He shared with me his faith journey. Though he was a relatively new Christian, his faith was deeper and more profound than many I have encountered before and since. He also shared how his being the first and only believer in his family has strained his relationship with them. His mother actually said that she thought that he was crazy and had joined a cult. He struggled over how to be Christ to/for them since sharing Christ was not possible.

After we returned to the city, he asked me to have dinner with him. Still, I asked God to protect our hearts, for I didn't want to rush heart-long into any infatuation that was not from God. I was cautious, and, it turns out, so was he. I was grateful for the ease of conversation and the common thread of wanting to serve God with our lives. He challenged me in his deep convictions and his passion.

This first dinner spilled over to many dates just the two of us, though we still enjoyed going out in groups with other fellow students. We usually walked to a nearby café and chatted until just before the last trains would run. Then I would call him from home, and we would talk for another half hour before saying "Goodnight" at midnight. I continued to pray over our relationship. I wanted to be pursued, but I wanted clarity. Until Taka finally asserted himself to tell me how he felt about me and that he wanted to pursue a relationship with me, I guarded myself and constantly brought my growing attraction for him to God.

When we finally told each other of our feelings and hopes and intentions for a relationship, I found out that he was in the same boat I was: wondering if this relationship was from God—not wanting any relationship to be short-term—but one that is meant to last. We prayed together for our relationship and asked God's blessings on each other.

From that point onward, though we were a couple, we still tried to be as discreet as possible and to focus on our studies and other activities. I think I filled my time to help me not to become too obsessed with my growing love for Taka. I knew that no mere man could be my "world" – a mentality that has helped me to have emotional balance.

During all those early months of our courtship, nearly every email from my parents had been filled with negativity voiced by other people from their church – mainly saying that Taka was only interested in me for getting a Green Card since he was Japanese. Finally, in discouragement and frustration, I asked Mom and Dad to tell me their own thoughts – because their opinion was more important to me than those of other people. Their response was a huge blessing – greater than I could have expected: "We have prayed a number of years for your future husband – now we will insert Taka's name as we continue to pray." God is *so* good!

A poem I composed in my journal around that time:

Precious

Trudging along this path
Following God and what He has planned
Looking ahead I hear a rustle
Turning to see you walking beside
Our hands collide, fingers
Intertwine to clasp and
Together we continue the path.

With you I'm cherished,
Wanted, desired,
By you I'm blessed
Encouraged and overwhelmed
By the Maker who saw
All along and merged
My path with yours
Together we journey
Together we pray
Together, I want us to stay.

Taka and I had a very brief romance, but it felt so much longer – deep and pure. We shared the same desire to be doing what we were called to do. We did not want to wait to finish the steps one by one. Of course, now, we can say that we are grateful for the time we spent completing the course and for all the faith challenges that we both faced during this time. It was difficult to know that he would graduate and I would still have another year of school and my compulsory internship before we could even decide on where and what and how. The first hurdle we must face together was choosing to continue our relationship while apart.

As the semester came to an end, I had to return to America and Taka was graduating and exploring his options for ministry. He applied to join MedAir (a disaster-relief organization based out of Switzerland). In the interim, his spiritual mentor hired him as a custodian at his church in Regina, Saskatchewan. We knew that God was first, and we vowed to keep Him in the center of our relationship. We agreed that our relationship was not a mistake and that it was worth fighting for. We said our farewell with many unknowns about our future together. In spite of all the miles between us and the uncertainty of Taka's location/placement, we continued to keep in touch through email and phone calls.

Chapter 6

A Summer and then a World Apart

I returned home at the end of the first full week of May. Everything felt out of place—myself, especially. I struggled with the feeling of being displaced all the more in realizing that I was detached and yet, my parent's place was still the only thing that I could call *home*. It was unsettling, to say the least. But, in retrospect, it was probably God working in my heart to get me ready for the life He had intended for me. I was not meant to stay. I was meant to go.

My best friend and I planned another week-long vacation, this time we flew to the West coast. Though we spent our time doing touristy things, we were also intentional with having deep conversations. We were both dating and we had similar issues that we were struggling with: "Is this man *the one?*," etc. It was a time of refreshing encouragement that I dearly needed as I waded through some major emotions regarding my calling and my growing love for Taka.

Throughout the summer, Taka and I maintained communication, in large part through email and then a phone call once or twice a week. We were serious about pursuing our relationship and also sensitive to what God was pulling each of us to. Taka was quite disappointed when the seminary wouldn't allow him to go through the CMA accreditation process because he was Japanese and was not even thinking of immigrating to Canada. I was still in line for accreditation the following year and we thought it best for me to continue the path that had been laid before me. As for Taka, he was unsettled about any future he had with the CMA.

In the meantime, I was back on the payroll at the Christian Bookshop where I had worked before I started seminary. I also continued attending the Bible study for young professionals and university students at another church. And yet, I still struggled with complacency and apathy. I couldn't understand how I could be so fickle in my faith. This complacency or dryness poured over into the way I communicated with Taka. I hated myself for it and I cried out to God to bring me out.

In the meantime, a month after I returned to the states, Taka was preparing for a short trip to Britain for his MedAir orientation and interview. This was a time for him to discern whether this was the path he should take and in what capacity. And though I prayed for him, I struggled with what this new assignment would do to our relationship. At times the distance seemed too overwhelming.

Taka was accepted and received notice of his proposed position as a volunteer logistician. It was a one-year commitment to start with. While waiting for his placement, he would continue to work at the church in Regina for a minimum of 3 months. And if I had any concerns about where our relationship was going, this was about the same time that we both wrote "I love you" in our emails to each other for the first time and started talking about life and ministry together.

Be that as it may, I struggled emotionally. Having this bright hope of talking about our future together spurred on my desire to get married – the sooner the better! I did not want to wait for 2 years (which, at the time, was the earliest that we could possibly get married due to our obligations: for me to finish school and for him to finish his one-year contract with MedAir).

It was a summer of waiting, pining, tears and frustration. I was given much encouragement, though, through Taka, through my best friend and in my Bible reading. Taka never sugar-coated things and always faced issues he noticed straight on. This did not always go very well with my pride, but I knew that when he pointed out my weaknesses, that it was out of love and desire for me to grow in character.

Toward the end of the summer, I contacted the CMA representative who was following my path. I asked him about my relationship with Taka and he confirmed that if I were to be a missionary with the CMA, Taka would have to be licensed by the CMA as well. That meant that if Taka wanted to be sent together with me that he would need to establish his residency in America with at least a Green Card. Otherwise, the only other foreseeable option was for him to go back to Japan and get established in a CMA church and go through the process there. It all just seemed impossible, but we believed that God still put us together for His purpose. And our love for each other grew.

In a way, I was angry. I was angry that there didn't seem to be anyone willing to work with us and for us. I knew that our situation was considered special circumstances, but also knew that with our situation, it would mean more "work" in terms of filing and registering, etc. In a way I was ashamed that the organization wouldn't deign to commit to helping us to go when we had been hearing over and over how few workers there were and that they were needing many more. We were there, saying, "Send us!" but because we didn't *fit*, we were summarily dismissed unless we were willing to wait and jump through all the hoops to become "acceptable" as a one-passport-couple. Admittedly, I struggled with this restrictive approach (though I do understand that requires more work behind the scenes). I never resented Taka. We were in this together. We were a packaged deal. But we began to see that the CMA would not be the path to travel. Now, don't get me wrong, the CMA is a wonderful organization and has done much in world missions, but it was discouraging that our situation was refused consideration.

By mid-August, Taka had received his placement with MedAir in North Sudan. A week after this news, my mom helped me drive up to Canada. We planned our route to go to Regina where I would visit with Taka and my mom could meet him (and hopefully give her approval). Mom stayed a few nights, attending church with Taka and me and spending time with Taka when he wasn't working. She left for Missouri by plane, giving us her blessing of approval of Taka. I spent a couple more days in Regina, visiting with Taka and having long talks about the future. We both admitted that though the future wasn't totally clear, we were still committed to each other and our relationship and that we were willing to wait and trust in God's timing.

Since I still had two semesters of school and an internship besides, I turned all my focus onto my studies. I don't think I ever truly gave my best effort to school until that time – I was so enthralled with what I was learning – it was an amazing and faith-building time in my life. Taka and I continued our emails and long-distance phone calls and we would hint at working in ministry together once his year-long commitment was finished at MedAir.

In the meantime, my candidate officer from the CMA advised me to apply for accreditation. I was conflicted. I had originally sought this wholeheartedly, but when I knew that there was no future for Taka with the CMA (at least not at this time), I felt that it was not something I wanted to pursue. I didn't want to be accredited only to change my mind. I wanted to commit for life for whatever it was that God was calling me to.

Around the same time, a fellow classmate once said that sometimes it is necessary to go, to begin the process of going before God's plan becomes clear. Taka and I talked a lot about this and he encouraged me to continue the process with the CMA until I felt that God was clearly leading me otherwise. My mind was going crazy, running all kinds of schemes that would always end with Taka and me together – married and in ministry overseas together. I felt lost in the quagmire of manmade regulations for sending missionaries. I was frustrated at the way things have been made so complicated with rules. I was a bit petulant, even. All in all, my journals were filled with so many different tangents and ideas, yet they always ended with "But not my will, Father, Yours be done."

Understandably, I was frustrated with not knowing exactly where Taka stood with this whole process. Then, in an email about a month after his departure, he wrote that his desire was that I would join him in whatever ministry he was involved in. This was what I needed to hear. Something more concrete—showing me that he was indeed thinking of our future together. It didn't matter how or with what organization—it just mattered that we were together serving the Lord.

After Christmas with my family, I returned to Calgary for my third semester. At the end of the first month, I flew again to Missouri to attend my best friend's wedding. It was a joy to have the shared experience with someone I love so dearly. At the same time, I pined for just such an occasion for Taka and me.

Around this time, there was a worship song that really spoke to my heart.

"If You Say Go"[7]

If You say, "Go," we will go

If You say "Wait," we will wait

If You say, "step out on the water"

---

[7] Rachel Milstead, "If You Say Go", Album *If You Say* Go, Vineyard Music, 2002.

And they say, "it can't be done"

We'll fix our eyes on You and we will come

    Your ways are higher than our ways

    And the plans that You have laid are good and true

    If You call us to the fire

    You will not withdraw Your hand

    We'll gaze into the flames and look for You.

Our relationship was very special and unique. It didn't fit any mold of anyone that I had known. Many people didn't really understand. Especially those from my parent's church, who would still submit their unwelcomed comments disparaging of Taka. One even went so far as to say something to the effect that I would change my mind once I met the new music minister at their church. I was hurt and offended by this, that anyone would think that I could be so fickle in my heart and with my affections. I brought the matter to Taka and he very wisely told me to disregard anything that we know is not truth. We continued to remain steadfast in our prayers for each other and worked at keeping open communication.

Still, I kept working through the different scenarios in which we could feasibly get married and go overseas as missionaries — which is what we were praying and hoping for. The options were varied and one of the following ideas would actually be that which God would lead us through:

1) I leave the CMA and go with him with MedAir
2) We leave our current 'organizations' and either go it on our own (<u>not</u> what I wanted to do) or find another organization to be sent by.

3) He applies to be sent to the same location I am with the Japan CMA.

4) He tries to work a 'deal' with the US-CMA where it would appear he is a resident but sent out as a missionary and in 5 years' time be able to apply for citizenship and we would be in the clear as far as being sent together without any 'strings' dangling.

In February of 2005, I had my accreditation interview and I was approved for licensing with the CMA pending the completion of my internship. Though I was relieved with this status with the CMA, I was still not comfortable with pursuing it. However, I continued my studies in earnest and started pursuing options for my intercultural internship.

Usually, the school finds locations to send its students to. However, seeing as I was an American in a Canadian school, I proved to be a bit of a quandary for the internship department. One of my professors had connections in the Philippines as a module teacher at their CMA seminary in Manila. He put the bug in my ear to check into the possibility of doing my internship at a CMA church there, as well as take the last required course for my degree program at the Manila campus.

Though the internship committee chairman did not like the idea, he failed to provide an alternative and I began making plans to go to the Philippines, as well as applied to the seminary for the course I needed to graduate. Since Taka was planning to spend a month in Japan at the end of his one-year commitment with MedAir, we began to tentatively make plans for me to join him there at the end of my 5-month internship in the Philippines.

Once I had approval, I reached out to the church in Manila and introduced myself. I didn't know the turmoil that I had unleashed in this simple act, but I was told that I would have a mentor and also accommodations with a family in the congregation. I also contacted

48

the seminary to register for the final course I needed for my degree. Everything was falling into place. I purchased a one-way ticket to the Philippines and began preparation for finals and packing.

As things started winding down for the semester, I began following up with finding out about other organizations by which Taka and I might be able to be sent. However, in the questionnaires, I found that there were other *requirements* that I had not considered before: the subject of home church. While I was at seminary, my parent's church was closed, and they were helping with a new church plant. My allegiance with the church in Canada was not solid, and Taka's home church was in Regina. And this is not to mention that we didn't have a home church to speak of as a couple. So...yet again, I was slapped with the realization that we just don't *fit* into the neatly prepared "box."

Be that as it may, Taka was also of the mind to pursue our options for being sent together by any other organization. We didn't have a particular timeframe, but we wanted to understand our options and start making plans. We were also of the same mind about fundraising. Neither one of us particularly enjoyed this aspect that is usually so ingrained in serving overseas. We both felt that if we were to truly be missionaries, that our faith to go would be confirmed by God providing for us. We, of course, would ask for prayer partners, for we know that as part of the body of Christ, having prayer support was much more necessary and way more powerful than financial. We know the reality of finances and their place and necessity, but we did not believe that we had to base our ability to go on funds alone.

A few days before the semester ended and as I was packing up my room to prepare for the drive back to the states, Taka sent me a series of emails in rapid succession asking for me to call him. With the tone of the emails leading up to this point, I was rather hopeful where the conversation would go. And I was so blessed by his beautiful request.

April 23, 2005: [PHONE CALL]:

[T]: [I] wanted to wait until November for this conversation, but felt that [we] needed to talk about this now – to make sure about our relationship.

[First of all, I am] poor and I can't give material [things]

[I] want to experience together God working in our lives and around us.

All the while he was fumbling with the right words, the growing hope in my heart and I was not disappointed! I enthusiastically and wholeheartedly accepted his proposal to marry him!

Chapter 7

Engagement, Wedding Plans and an Internship

With this euphoria of a definite answer to my own desires, my mind went into hyper drive with all the details to consider. First of all, I needed to focus enough attention to finish my degree program well: which meant taking my last required classes at the seminary in Manila and completing a 5-month internship at a CMA church there.

Once the news of our engagement spread among friends and relatives, I started working on how things would unfold. We did not want to wait too much longer after we were to meet in Japan in November. We had a big hurdle to decide on: the when and where of our wedding. In a matter of days I had considered and discarded more than a dozen schemes ranging from getting married overseas in Japan, to marrying in an intermediary location like Hawaii where everyone could meet us halfway, to getting married in Missouri where most of my family could join and celebrate the day with us.

When I got back to Missouri, I had about a month to plan the wedding, dress, etc. before heading to the Philippines. My mom helped pick out a simple wedding dress pattern which she would make from satin she had bought and been saving for just this special occasion, and my dad took me to several chapels/churches to choose for the ceremony (their church had closed and was then meeting in a school cafeteria). In the end, I decided on the Old Peace Chapel on the Daniel Boone Homestead in Defiance, Missouri.

Once these major decisions were made, I felt more at ease to allow my mom some freedom-within-reason with the rest of the details (at the time I was adamant that my dress be simple and elegant and was often heard saying, "No beads, no bows, no buttons, no lace!"). I did the research on the timeframe for changing my IDs and my parents presented us with a honeymoon getaway gift. With all this, it was decided to get married on December 17th. Until we had a solid direction and path before us, we would stay in my parent's basement in a newly renovated suite. With this in mind, I left to start my internship.

My time in the Philippines was spent in study and teaching the youth Sunday school and forming the youth activities. The time passed slowly with its share of trials: 1) some board members didn't want me there (reasons still unknown); 2) three times money went missing from my room – a total of $500 and; 3) dealing with cultural barriers that would teach me to be humbler in any approach to ministry, etc.

Aside from those trials and tests of my faith, the internship did hold many lessons that would shape my faith and my worldview as I prepared for a life overseas. I had a lot of arrogance in some areas regarding my capabilities and I was not prepared for the amount of humility I would need to endure in terms of what I believed I was capable of and what was entrusted to me. Looking back, I can see just how this really shaped my heart to cull out my propensity for being results-oriented. Ministry is about the hearts of the people and caring for sick hearts…something that takes time, years even.

And there I was, arrogant to think that 5 months would even have any kind of lasting impact beyond merely scratching the surface. I was still learning that any short-term ministry is more about self-development and shaping than for the benefit of the people I am presumptuous enough to claim I was helping. Yes, I did my best to help where I was tasked, but in the large scheme of things, this 5 months, just like the 9-10 months in Siberia, was more for my own spiritual formation and solidify growing my faith in God. It was also a tool He used to solidify His calling on my life and His blessing on my relationship with Taka as our romance continued in earnest by emails and occasional phone calls throughout this time.

As I mentioned, I experienced having money stolen from me. $400 of the $500 was taken from my room within the first 3 weeks. The first time was within the first week and I searched my whole room several times but kept the story to myself. When it happened the second time (each time $200 was taken), I let my host family know and gave them what cash I had left to keep in their safe. I did not share about this missing money with very many people because I didn't want misunderstanding or undue mistrust to occur. Out of the remaining funds I had prepared and brought with me, more than 2/3rds was needed for expenses of tuition and visa. Still, it was discouraging to hear from my mentor that there were slanderous rumors being spread about me and how much money I had, etc. I shared openly with my mentor about the situation and asked for continued prayer over the matter and protection from this attack.

Meanwhile, in my off time when I wasn't preparing new youth study materials and resources, or working on assignments for my classes, I was continuing to research all mission-sending organizations, especially those working within Asia. I also brainstormed what I could do to further prepare for the field were we to end up staying in the US longer than we initially intended. I did not have much experience in many practical things, so I started considering going back to school to learn a trade like midwifery or nursing, etc.

My time in the Philippines did have its share of encouragement. I was paired with another missionary to act as an accountability partner and she, together with my mentor, challenged me and spurred me on in my spiritual walk. They called me on some of my mess and helped me through some of the issues I struggled with during my internship, my studies, my questioning about the direction for Taka and me to take, niggling doubts about not having the support of either a home church or a sending organization, etc. Even my CMA representative reinforced the fact that God knew when He called Taka and me that we would go through these steps and struggles of wandering and wondering

One of the issues that left us wondering was regarding the type of visa that Taka would travel to the US on since we were intending to get married. According to the law, one would have to apply for a tourist visa since it is one of the types that is eligible to change the status of. Applying for a fiancé visa was out of the question owing to our very peculiar situation. That, and the fact that it was a 6-12 month process. And if he chose to go to the States on the 90-day visa waiver, he could be brought up on fraud charges because most of the foreigners who get married to US citizens are intending to do so in order to immigrate to the States. So, we kind of looked at this predicament as a clear sign for us to go soon after our wedding (within 2 months) rather than stay in the states until "something came up."

I wrapped up my internship with a youth retreat with all the youth cell groups coming together for a trip to Banawe to see some famous rice terraces. I also attended a Women's Conference with several ladies from the church. My last act as an intern was two-fold: I was challenged to lead the Tagalog-speaking service in worship, and I turned over my packet of resources I had been building for discipleship of youth. As I was approaching my departure, I decided to do some last-minute souvenir shopping for the people who were helping with our wedding. That was when the last $100 was taken from my room, when I had left my room without locking it. I can tell you, I was enraged and also shocked. But in the end, there was nothing more I could do about the situation except to simply hand it over to God and to move forward. It hurt that my privacy was invaded within the house of my hosts. And trying to guess who was responsible was just as infuriating and pointless.

Finally, the end came, and I was reunited with Taka in Japan, where we spent the next month visiting with his parents and sister and getting better acquainted as an engaged couple. We talked about our options to be sent as missionaries, but there seemed to be roadblocks at every turn. With the already troubling and lengthy process delaying the possibility of being sent by the CMA, we set aside any thoughts of pursuing this as a possibility for us.

Our next hurdle was the fact that we wanted to be sent as soon as possible, but all the organizations we approached had requirements in place that prevented us from even applying: 1) we were different nationalities with no intention of pursuing naturalization (either for Taka to become American or me, Japanese); 2) We had no 'real' church home, either as individuals or as a couple (as explained earlier) and; 3) we were just about to be married and no organization would agree to have a 1st-year married couple sent to any field.

Throughout our month in Japan, we spent a lot of time discussing our vision for the future and our desires for ministry. Our conversations included Cambodia as a possibility. We both knew a missionary working there, and Taka also had a strong connection to the country because that was where he came to know Christ and had some connections with other missionaries there as well.

However, there were still some people in our lives that would rather we do anything BUT be missionaries. My parents, though emotionally sad over the fact that I was intending for a life overseas, were still supportive of our decision to follow wherever God was leading. Having Taka in my life to go with me gave my mom a peace since I was not going alone. However, not everyone was as supportive. Lifelong friends of the family and even new friends had their own ideas of how we could still serve God while staying close to home. Even Taka's mother went so far as to say that she would buy us an apartment and that she would open up some kind of shop and hire me to be her staff – just so that we could stay close by. Traditionally, it is the oldest son who stays in the parents' home and looks after them in their old age—and Taka is the *only* son. This has been a "bone of contention" for some time. And though we have her approval as a family, we have weathered her disappointment over our choice to live overseas over the years. Taka is also the first Christian in his family, which leads to their inability to understand or share in the vision that we have to live overseas as missionaries.

Being faced with such a responsibility to follow his mother's wishes and following God was not something Taka took lightly. Taka loves his family and prays diligently for them to receive Christ. But he cannot deny the calling on our lives, even in light of the disappointment he must face in his mother's eyes. However, Taka did impart the promise that were his parents' health ever to reach the point when they would need his presence that he would be faithful to care for them within his power to do so.

"A person who lives in faith must proceed on incomplete evidence, trusting in advance what will only make sense in reverse." –Philip Yancey[8]

[8] Yancey, Philip. *Reaching For The Invisible God: What Can We Expect To Find?* Zondervan, 2000.

Chapter 8

From the Wedding to Overseas

$\mathscr{A}$fter just over four weeks in Japan, Taka and I went to Missouri. We had 10 days to apply for the marriage license and finalize all wedding plans. This included making sure that Taka's spiritual mentor and pastor came from Canada to perform the ceremony. On December 17, 2005, we got married in the Old Peace Chapel on the Daniel Boone Homestead in Defiance, Missouri. I remember being blessed that most of our closest relatives and family friends surrounded us at the end of the ceremony to pray over us and bless us.

We finalized the day with a relaxed reception at my parents' home with more friends coming to celebrate our wedding. Some people were there that I would never meet again on this earth, among them was my Grandmother, (my dad's mother). By then her Alzheimer's was progressing and her childlike joy was a blessing to see. We laughed like little girls over little things and she was in good spirits and enjoyed reintroducing herself to the same people throughout the day.

My brother and his daughter also came, which was an added blessing since I had not seen my brother since the summer before I went to Kyzyl. And my Grandma. She seemed so tiny and fragile, but I remember sitting with her on the sofa in my parents' family room, taking in the people-watching together and enjoying the quiet companionship shrouded in peace and joy.

Truth be told, I remember simply spending unhurried times of conversation with the people who came. After ending the reception with cake and final hugs all around, Taka and I headed out for our honeymoon. We spent a week at Big Cedar Lodge in Branson, MO. It was over this time that we had a clear connection on our agreement that we each desired to go *now* rather than wait and jump through man's imposed hoops. We came away from that week with a fierce focus on making that happen.

We spent Christmas with my parents and then went to my Grandma's house to spend the week after Christmas. It was during this week that we were able to meet with some friends from Canada and had a very encouraging chat with them about what we were thinking in terms of our next steps toward fulfilling the call on our hearts for overseas missions. On the car ride back to my Grandma's house after meeting them, we had a chat and I proposed that we simply say that we are going and commit, and that God would work out the rest.

Over the next couple of weeks, Taka contacted his missionary friends in Cambodia who assured us that we would be welcomed and needed (despite the fact that we didn't have a specific work to do or even have an organization we would be affiliated with).

Since Taka's visa would expire the beginning of March, we decided to make a trip to Canada to visit our pastors there. What we received from that visit was priceless. They blessed us with a spiritual sending prayer and commissioning service. Though they could not endorse us through their denomination, they saw that we were committed to the call we had, and they sent us with their prayers, their encouragement and their hearts. It was more than I ever expected to receive. We were overwhelmed by God's great mercy and grace over us to wipe out any doubts as to His plan for us to go at that time.

As we continued talking and dreaming about the impending relocation to Cambodia, we still didn't have a clear vision for the work that God was preparing us for. I recall that during one of my visits to Taka in Regina that someone prophesied over me that this person saw me surrounded by a bunch of children; by orphans. I remember at the time thinking, ok—are you sure? Even with that prophecy, I still did not have any clarity. Taka and I wanted to have a ministry unique to us – one that was totally dependent on God working through us as He led. After a week of spiritual replenishment and encouragement, we headed back to Missouri to finalize our plans for getting to Cambodia and what that entailed.

On the way back by bus, we found out much more as to the discrepancies and legality of our marriage and just how serious this is taken through an unfortunate incident when we reached the Canada/ US border to re-enter the US. We had submitted a family customs form while I was still traveling under my maiden name. This led to an hour-long interrogation by the border US customs officer.

The main reason for the interrogation was to figure out if we were indeed committing fraud. Taka was on the wrong kind of visa. It didn't matter that we had a legal marriage license or the fact that Taka and I have no intention of living in the US, much less his immigrating to the US. It was quite intimidating. The officer separated us and questioned us regarding our *story* to see if what we said would match up. I remember praying over and over for us to find favor and that I would not break down in tears. At one point the main interrogator accused me of lying because Taka was giving him different answers. When they finally released us, we found out that he wasn't even asking us the same questions.

As soon as we got back to Missouri, I applied to have my name changed on my Social Security card, Driver's license and applied for a new passport. I had already sold my car – which, when budgeted with other monetary wedding gifts, would afford us a meager living to last roughly 2 years in Cambodia. Taka and I continued talking about what fears, concerns, dreams and desires we had, especially how we desired for God to give us the clear path.

Taka bought his ticket back to Japan to set things in order there while I awaited the turnaround on my documents with my new name. He would also make the necessary arrangements for our approaching arrival to Cambodia by reaching out to his contacts. During this time of preparation leading up to his departure, I had a dream that I was surrounded by clamoring children. It was brief and I awoke wondering about it, and the memory of being prophesied over came flooding back as it seemed to be the same.

After Taka left, I tried to make the best of my time with Mom and Dad. I wanted to leave them with memories of our time together in those few days because there was no telling what kind of communication we would be able to have. We also had no idea when I would see them again. We had no fixed plan. We had no official organizational backing. We answered only to God. In a way, it was daunting. But what outweighed it was the unmistakable feeling of freedom in being able to move and live as God would lead us. We prayed constantly that we would live to honor Him and His calling on us. And His peace continually flooded my heart as I continued to lay everything at His feet.

I wrapped up my time in Missouri and packed as frugally as I could, especially since we planned to travel to Cambodia through Thailand. There was a new budget airline that was advertising fares at a great discount from Bangkok to Phnom Penh. The catch was that each passenger would only be allowed one 15kg checked bag and one carry-on weighing 7kg (about 33lbs and 15lbs respectively). I joined Taka in Japan where we spent nearly three weeks of final preparations.

It was during these weeks in Japan that I first noticed how skewed my attention and focus had gotten in terms of how I saw myself as a woman. I put an expectation on our relationship and projected that Taka would fulfill me as a woman – something that God never intended. I questioned everything and had an outward perspective, making myself the victim or the innocent. I'm not even sure what it was that I wanted Taka to do or say, but I know that I was not satisfied with what he was doing and saying and I didn't know how to reconcile what I felt I was being denied.

Though I continually brought these new, strange, and rather discouraging thoughts to God, I still continued to look to Taka

– how he interacted with me, etc, to be the barometer to measure
my worth. This would be a constant inward contention for the first
six moths of married life and time in Cambodia. Not as glorious
as I had painted in the picture in my head.

After spending three weeks with his parents and a couple of
days being tourists in Bangkok, we landed in Cambodia on March
18, 2006 – three months and a day after we had gotten married.

For the first week and a half we stayed with a missionary
friend of Taka's. Thinking back to our first week in Cambodia
when we were still staying in the spare bedroom, we did a lot of
soul-searching. I remember one particular night while lying awake,
we turned to each other and we both had the same thought: "Now
what?" Thus started intensive prayer for direction as to what God
had in store for us. Taka and I scouted out the area and found an
apartment to rent. I also found a language school and we enrolled
in 1-on-1 tutoring starting April 3rd.

Over the next few months, we visited several different organizations to talk with seasoned missionaries and to hear of the work
that they were doing. We wanted to learn for ourselves what the
needs of this nation were and what God was calling us to do. We
also had several offers to join the work that was already in progress.
One offer was to spearhead the first initiative of an international
organization in Phnom Penh. I'll admit that we had our own "blue
sky" dreams, but none of the offers we received really pricked our
hearts to take the plunge.

We were also quite discouraged, and even annoyed, by the per-
spectives of some missionaries and their opinions of the general
Cambodian populace. We didn't want to have a biased or skewed
view of the people we were being called to serve before we got to
know them personally. We agreed that we would not internalized
any negative comments because we knew that God has called us
to love others. How could we love the people of Cambodia if we

were taking the words of others without experiencing firsthand for ourselves?

Therefore, we decided to focus on our language studies, committing to at least 2 years of focused learning: learning about the people, the culture, the way things are and how we can partner to do whatever it would be that God was calling us to do. We did agree to join one organization to teach English 4 nights a week and to join in their Bible studies and Sunday services as they reached the very students that they were teaching English to.

All the while, we were still waiting. We felt that God was calling us to something "new" and we were disenchanted by some initiatives that left a gap between the workers and the people they were serving. We definitely did not want there to be a gap.

Our first few months were difficult for me. Taka seemed to hit his rhythm and stride much quicker than I did, and I was frustrated with constant fatigue and then followed a severe chest cold that lasted 2 weeks. Those first few months were also riddled with great expectations that were thwarted by self-doubt. I was in a battlefield; one in which my mind and thought life were constantly warring between elation and purpose to disenchantment and self-deprecation. We both had good language days and bad. But one thing we did learn is that our individual learning styles were *not* compatible. Since we also had different teachers, the way he learned some things did not make sense to me. So we couldn't even quiz each other on certain aspects of our language learning. I had a trained school teacher, who would give me written tests and challenged me to translate and to write stories and songs. Taka's teachers were more relaxed and allowed him to lead the direction he would take.

We were struggling individually and also as a couple. We had never had a lot of face-to-face time in our courtship. In fact, from the time we started dating until we said, "I do," we spent only five out of the 22 months together in person. Now here we were in a foreign country, trying to build our relationship but without a community to call our own. We were definitely unprepared for the sense of alienation we experienced. For me, it was a time of calling out to God constantly and fighting against the level of dependency I was falling into, which only caused more trouble. It took months for me to pull myself up and to strike out independently beyond the familiar places.

I had an idea in my head that we would do things together. Taka expressed the same sentiment, but our definitions of "together" were different. So, though we were saying the same word, we had different expectations of ourselves and each other. For me, it meant to do each process together and have input from each other on the important things. For him, it was to divide and conquer a common goal; working independently, but getting more work done.

I didn't discover this until much later. If I had, I would have probably spared myself much heartache and second-guessing. I would not have been in such emotional turmoil. I remember one time lying on our one-meter cotton mattress weeping for our relationship. Taka, who had been studying his language lesson, came over to ask me what was wrong. But I really couldn't find the words to describe what I was feeling and told him that I didn't know what to say. Feeling rather helpless to comfort me, he let me alone. And I cried all the more with this perceived rejection by the one I wanted to simply wrap his arms around me and hold me in that time of desperation.

On another note, Taka is a much more studious person that I am. He is also *very* focused. I, however, am too easily distracted. I knew that when he was on the computer or reviewing, that it was important to him to not be interrupted. But I had a misconception that he took way too much time on studies and I got the meager leftovers. I wanted more of him.

On the other hand, it was going through this that helped bind us together as a couple so that we could move forward, completely united in Christ. It also taught me the importance of fighting for our marriage in the spiritual realm by praying against these mental and emotional attacks and laying our relationship at the altar, trusting that God doesn't make mistakes. There was much soul-searching, and also re-learning to put my all in Jesus and to allow God His proper place in my heart: *First*.

All the while, we were constantly praying and wondering about our own unique ministry. After several months of waiting and seeking, Taka received a vision and a heart to focus on disadvantaged children in Cambodia. We visited and took notes from other like-minded missionaries and their work. We also saw a myriad of NGOs (non-government organizations) already working in Phnom Penh, so we began searching for a place that had no existing NGO; in particular, existing orphanage. My language teacher's older brother was founder of a local NGO, so we began talking with them about how to go about registering and receiving a permit to do what we felt called to do. It was then suggested that instead of waiting for all the red tape that we simply come under their umbrella organization as one of their projects.

Through my language teacher and her family, we began inquiring about finding a piece of land that met our stipulations where we would build our first home to welcome orphans and disadvantaged children. For our philosophy or theology of ministry, there were some very important stands we wanted to make: 1) to be Christ-centered – keeping Him in focus 100% of the time, not falling into the trap of focusing more on the work than on Him; 2) to provide for the spiritual, as well as basic life and educational needs of all children who would come to us and; 3) to raise children in a family (however big) that understands God's saving grace and unconditional love.

Initially, the vision was so vast that we knew that we could not do it all alone. We began praying for partners in the work to be able to see the whole vision realized. With our sights set on a potential property, we envisioned having our house and dormitories-both for small kids and for youth of both genders, a large covered play area, outside washing areas for laundry, additional buildings for studying, visiting teams, staff, community outreach to house elderly and/or widows with no one to depend on, and, of course, a chapel for worship and Bible teaching. It seemed a grandiose vision for such as us – having absolutely *NO* background or experience in any aspect of this undertaking, but we were so excited to see how God would flesh out this vision.

"So will My word be which goes forth from My mouth; it will not return to Me empty, without accomplishing what I desire, and without succeeding in the matter for which I sent it.

For you will go out with joy and be led forth with peace; the mountains and the hills will break forth into shouts of joy before you, and all the trees of the field will clap their hands."

-Isaiah 55:11-12

Chapter 9

Vision, Laying the Groundwork, Among Other Things

*N*ow that we had a clear direction, we needed to figure out the next steps. My language teacher and her extended family were indispensable in this process. We talked at length with them about what we felt God was calling us to do. We didn't want to be "just another orphanage" among the many. We wanted to be different. We also didn't want to be in too close a proximity with a similar work or focus. So, we turned our attention to finding land in one of the provinces.

Before our search really got off the ground, though, Taka received a phone call from Japan. His mother had suffered a major stroke and was hospitalized. At first her prognosis seemed relatively light, but after feeling compelled to go to Japan, Taka soon found out the severity of her situation. She was paralyzed on her left side and would spend many months in the hospital learning to function in her new capacity. He left to be with her for 6 weeks while I remained in Cambodia.

What he found was devastating. His mother, a gregarious and very active person, was now faced with a lifestyle change that she could not control. She took great courage while Taka stayed with her in the hospital, reading to her, talking to her, praying for her. He cared for her in her needs and helped to dispel her depression as she came to terms with her physical disabilities. It was a key time in their relationship as he ministered to her and loved on her. He and his father spent a lot of time going through the montage of papers that she had filed unbeknownst to his father. He was also able to help with some of the major decisions about preparing for her eventual discharge from the hospital.

About the time of Taka's departure to Japan to be with his family, my language teacher's brother, a pastor in Kampong Cham Province, started scouting properties that met our prerequisites: 1) no existing NGO and; 2) near local schools and market. So, every weekend, I went to see a few properties with my teacher and her brother. I made note of all the places that showed promise and added them to a short list that Taka and I would revisit. When he returned, we went, and prayerfully considered.

When I wasn't taking day tours of different properties or attending my Khmer lessons or teaching English, I fell into a pattern of laziness when at home. I developed a very unhealthy habit of watching movies non-stop while in the home. I was lonely, yet I was not taking any initiative to make an effort to do anything. In a way, I used the TV as a distraction for my solitude and loneliness. I hated myself. I battled with the self-directed anger over my slothfulness, yet I continued to pick up that TV remote every time I woke up, every time I entered our apartment. A journal entry from that time:

December 3, 2006:

Lord, all this time I have fallen farther and farther away – throwing myself to diversions – wasting hours and hours in front of the TV. I am sick of myself – and yet I am continually drawn – almost

70

to the point where it consumes me – even in the morning, I'm watching, in the afternoon – almost the first thing I'm doing is turning on the TV and plugging in a DVD. Oh Lord, break me! Even now! I want to be after You, Lord, in the same way – but even more so – as I have been drawn to the TV. I know why You have put Taka in my life – to be my mainstay – he is solid in his faith in You – to encourage, spur me on and continue to put my focus to You. I know that he cannot save me – only You! But what does it say of me that when he is not around that I crumble away so easily? I am human. I am a sinner. I am weak, Lord.

Lord, every moment of every day is about You – not me! Help me, Lord, to love You with all my heart, soul, mind, and strength!

Lord, I desire to walk with You as Noah did, to speak with You face-to-face as Moses did and to be a woman after Your heart as David and to choose the greater things of You as Mary (Martha's sister) chose.

After following this pattern for some time, I determined to take a TV-sabbatical and it remained off the second half of Taka's absence. At first the silence was deafening. I tried to read my Bible, but would often get bored and start thinking of other things and doing other things. I borrowed novels to read, I played music, and I even started to exercise. But all these were futile attempts to run away from the one voice I needed most of all: God's. Finally, in desperation, I began setting small goals to make appointments with God throughout the days. And little by little, the dripping faucet began to trickle and pour. It was during this time that I was able to really focus on hearing God's voice and reconnecting and realigning my heart to His.

And God spoke to my heart – right to the core of the issues. He began untangling the misplaced reliance I had on Taka to turn it back to Him. In the six months that we had been in Cambodia, I had become much too dependent on Taka, to the point where I was heavily relying on him to give me affirmation instead of turning to God. By God's grace, the time of Taka's return was a celebration for both of us. God worked in our hearts individually while apart, so that, when we reunited, we were in a better heart-condition and able to reconnect in a way that was deeper and more committed than before. We still had to learn and relearn to let go of unmet expectations and to simply be and to love and to encourage one another, but the time of separation worked in a positive way to bring us closer together than before.

Right after Christmas, we received our first guests from "home." These dear friends came to encourage us for nearly two weeks over the New Year. It was a blessing for me to have someone here to simply pour into our hearts and to be an encouragement to us. Their visit was, in a way, healing to me. They really ministered to us and asked us to tell them what all we were *not* sharing with our prayer supporters in our newsletters. And they listened, encouraged and prayed with us. It gave me clarity that we were truly in God's will and we were affirmed in the work that He was guiding us to, while being faithful to the goals and commitments we had made in the interim. Their visit replenished my heart that had been emptied for lack of community. Yes, I was integrating into a community, but I wasn't fully committed, which left me still on the outside and not united with other believers. Their visit also reawakened my burning desire to be used of God in any way.

As Taka and I continued to learn how to communicate and love each other well, I still struggled with misplaced perceptions of our interactions. I know that we both had our own ideas of what

we wanted the other to do, especially when it came to conversations. However, we were not meeting each other very well at times.
Sometimes when I was in the mood to chat, he was busy and vice
versa. Taka wanted to make the most of the daytime and filled it
well with studying the language. I know that there were times I did
not respect that and received a rebuff. Whenever that happened
early in our time in Cambodia, I would slink away to cry my heart
out to God asking, "Why?" I felt so rejected, so unloved. But over
time, I learned that there was a better way to approach Taka that
would nourish us both. However, that did not mean that I always
followed what I learned. After one such encounter, I turned to God
and journaled feverishly as I poured my heart out to Him:

February 3, 2007:

...Why is it that I am always making myself out to
be the victim when my feelings are hurt, Lord? I
know that my feelings are genuine – but are they
misplaced – are they swayed by the spirit or the
flesh? I know that Taka could never fulfill me or
complete me or meet all my needs...That is only
found in You and according to Your will and Your
knowing best for my needs. I thank You, Lord, that
You love me – even as often as I fall; when I look
up, I am in Your love. Father, forgive my misplaced
dependency → I can only be dependent on You. You
are my Rock!

Lord, who are You calling me to be? You are calling
me to be me.

Lord, what is my role –

Your role is, first of all, a daughter of God and
secondly a wife, a disciple, a learner, a sojourner

following the path that is set, committing all your ways to God and getting up when you fall. You are not alone. I have placed My Spirit within you and have chosen your companion to strengthen and encourage each other as you continue to follow Me – the path I set; the steps I order – to do the work of God with your lives.

Oh God – You are too wonderful for me! And yet, You chose me, love me, forgive me…

In March, we wrapped up our commitment for teaching English and looked forward to focusing more on realizing the vision God had given to us about opening a home for children. The nine months we spent teaching and working alongside this other organization was a time of much growth as we learned more about ourselves and different approaches to ministry.

We learned more about what our core values are and how we hoped to implement and live them out in the future of our ministry. Among the core values that came out was the reminder that all must be done in love. If there is no love, what kind of witness can we hope to have? We loved our students and we invested in them. We invited them to our home to play games and have deeper conversations. Relationships take time. Trust takes time. We built trust and enjoyed our relationships with the students even after we stopped teaching. Some students still came over to our house to play games and to talk in English. We also talked a lot about what questions they had about the God of our Bible, of our hearts. Some of our students came from a strong Buddhist background and were not allowed to attend Bible studies or church services, but they were still hungry and our open door allowed them a chance to learn more.

…

At the end of our commitment to teaching English, we made a plan to go to Japan to help Taka's father finalize the move to the new, handicap-accessible apartment that he had bought, as well as to be there when his mother would be discharged from rehabilitation. Our time in Japan was relatively quiet. Since the apartment was much smaller than their house, we helped to sort through their belongings. Taka spent most of the days at the hospital with his mother. There was little I could do, so I stayed mostly at the new apartment. At the end of six weeks, I returned to Cambodia alone while Taka stayed another month to help his mom integrate to their new home life and with her limited abilities for self-mobility. By God's grace, she was able to walk with assistance, but due to illness, had to prolong her stay in the hospital.

Once back in Cambodia, I had to reconcile with a new rhythm of life since I was no longer teaching English. I filled my time with visiting more properties in the provinces with my teacher and her family. I was also confronted with several strongholds and doubts I had been cultivating in my heart. I kept returning to the deteriorating habit of laziness. It was not present while Taka was around because I felt guilt. Left on my own, I would sink into the abyss of mindless entertainment to fill my days. I hated this about myself, but it was difficult to shake the hazy cobwebs that were clouding my mind. I was relying on my own efforts, and not turning to God.

April 5, 2007:

Lord, ... I'm consumed with myself – everyday. I step on the scale 3 or 4 times, I check my appearance many times; browse the shops coveting the clothes I can't afford; I'm consumed with what I think I deserve in reference to the treatment by others. Almost everything I've bought this last week was for me. What kind of person am I? Lord, show me Your ways that I may understand and know You! I am not favorable (and doubt I ever will be) but I want to find favor in <u>YOUR</u> eyes – not the eyes of the world… if only to bring glory to Your name. Are my words cheap? Maybe, because they fly up like the sparks from the fire, yet soon cool to the winds of the world. What am I to do? Help me to die to myself, LORD! I need <u>YOU</u>! I have no real strength in me. I have no power. It is only <u>YOU</u> who, while in me, working in me, has all the strength, power, wisdom, knowledge, love, truth, grace, goodness, faithfulness. Awake in me, oh my soul! Bring praise to His Name! Teach me, Lord. Teach me to serve You wherever You lead me – in every season, place and situation. I have become a slug here. Giving not even half my attention to You when I sit down to my devotion with You…am I merely doing it as a pretense? When Taka confronted me with "What did you do today," I immediately felt defensive – was it out of guilt for how little my life seems filled right now? As with everything when I am defensive, I justified myself. Why am I defensive? And yet, what am I justifying? My sloth?

I had to make a conscious choice to ignore the TV and to open my Bible and journal and to sit and read. Again, it was a slow restart. I began praying through the Psalms. God was working on me, and through seeking Him, I was able to realign myself to whom He has called me to be. My identity is in Him. He is with me. He has everything in the palm of His hand. I also continually learned to let go of what I thought I could control in our marriage.

With Taka's return, we found that the reality of our budget set aside for buying land was not realistic. After prayerfully considering our options: paying our original budget for less land or raising the budget to find a property that matched the vision we have been given, we decided to move in faith with the latter choice. With this new budget, our options seemed to multiply before us and we visited property after property, hoping that each one would prick our hearts and resonate with the vision God had given to us.

We also struggled in the "now" and "not yet" of this waiting period. We struggled with finding a property that encompassed the whole vision while chomping at the bit to finally get started with the work that we believed firmly and passionately that God was calling us to do. I did spend time struggling with God about the vision; was it from God or more from my flesh,and were there aspects that, if from the flesh, I would be willing to do without.

July 6, 2007:

"There's so much now I cannot see,

My eyesight's far too dim;

But come what may, I'll simply trust

And leave it all to Him."

-Overton[9]

Lord, help me to say the words above with all my heart – especially now when neither Taka nor I have any clear indication (that we can see) regarding any of the lands that we have seen thus far.

---

[9] From the poem by A. M. Overton, "He Maketh No Mistake", 1932

Added to all this was the decidedly different temperaments that Taka and I have for making decisions. Though I struggled with second-guessing my own decisions, I was still at peace about everything, knowing, through God's continual faithfulness, that all would work out when it would work out: according to His timing. There were times I made Taka very frustrated when I couldn't offer any definitive direction or decision about some of the BIG decisions we had to make. When I think back to this time, I recall that in high-intense situations God granted us the grace that only one of us would brood and worry while the other would remain in the assurance of His grace. This kept us balanced and still carries true even today.

August 3, 2007

Lord, is what I'm experiencing the 'calm before the storm?' Lord, I ask You to awaken me – jumpstart my heart! Where is my focus? What is my place, my part in my relationship with Taka, in this vision? I kind of feel 'left out' – he shares his vision from You, he leads, he has peace, and then here I am without a clear vision, without clarity of thought or purpose – I feel like I have become the club foot. I feel like I am holding Taka back. I feel so often that I am merely a distraction, a nuisance, and one who impedes our progress forward. Oh Lord, reconcile me to Your heart. Reveal to me the strongholds I have placed in my heart before You...

self-appearance

desire for "things"

desire for Taka...

Lord, I have put myself before You! Oh wretch that
I am! Help me to step back and away from Your
place – the center, the throne of my heart and life!

Finally, we found the property that spoke to our hearts and we
committed to its purchase. Being foreigners, we are not allowed
to officially own land in Cambodia, so any property would have to
be put in the name of someone we trusted. God provided the funds,
the land and the trusted friend. The property was in the commune
called Bos Khnor (meaning "jackfruit"), approximately 120km
(or 75mi) from the capital, Phnom Penh. It lay nestled between a
Chinese school and cashew plantations on three sides. By August,
we were able to purchase the land and pay the down payment for
the construction of the initial building. My teacher introduced us
to her brother-in-law who was a contractor and we made a contract with him.

In mid-August, Taka received word that his uncle had suffered
a stroke and Taka was requested to return to Japan to be with his
family. He booked a flight for himself while I opted to stay in
Cambodia now that things were starting to move with our property
purchase. For me, it was more out of self-preservation. Although I
did want to go to Japan in support of Taka, I recalled the last trip I
had taken and how useless and listless my days had become with
very little for me to do. By staying in Cambodia, I could at least
continue my integration into the Khmer culture, especially with the
very prominent fact that I would be the first white person living in
the location where our property was.

This is not to say that, despite our calling to Cambodia, that
Taka did not receive criticism from his family and relatives. When
he went to Japan, he was faced with the reality that most of his
relatives did not see the use of us living on what was deemed a
volunteering position in a country far from Taka's home. In fact, it
was intimated that since we weren't really "working" that it seemed

only fair that Taka and I move back to Japan to take care of his grandma now that his uncle had compromised health. Though Taka's father helped greatly with all the official forms and submission of documents on behalf of his brother-in-law, Taka's uncle. His efforts, though much-needed, were sadly construed as having ulterior motives since he was not a blood relative. However, other relatives were not actively helping in any matters at the same time that they were criticizing Taka for our lifestyle choice of living in Cambodia and "doing nothing but volunteer work." It was difficult for me to hear the struggle that Taka and his parents were having with the whole situation.

Meanwhile, in Cambodia, we were in the "hurry-up-and-wait" phase with the property and getting things off the ground. Once we had the title and the building permit, our contractor broke ground on the property in mid-October of 2007. As we took stock of our finances and the cost of everything that seemed to be piling up: from the purchase of the land, to the building our Taka-designed-building, and all the additional costs for furnishing and preparing for our impending move to the province, we found that we had just enough funds available in our bank accounts. And then God blessed us with a tremendous financial blessing — and from someone we didn't even know!

In mid-November, after construction on the property was underway, I made a surprise trip to the US. I called my mom from one of my transit stops to tell her that I was coming into town that night. I spent a wonderful month or so with my parents, my grandma and other friends and loved ones. It was a time well-cherished. I was filled with love and blessing from everyone and returned to Cambodia with a full heart. It was also to be the last time I would see my grandma, for she passed away in January of the following year. My response to her death was one of peace in spite of heartache. In the years since my time in Siberia, I had been more intentional in my conversations with her and God's peace encompassed me through the grieving – a time that was replenished with all the memories of our times together in recent years.

Since our property was in the province and a four-hour drive in a bus or minivan, Taka would commute to the property once or twice a week to see how progress was going. Upon my return, we found that there had been some miscommunication with the contractor. Therefore, Taka had to make some adjustments to the building plans to compensate for our own ignorance and to the miscommunication we were experiencing. We learned the hard way that if we want something done in a particular way, the power of physical presence makes all the difference — potentially a very tense and stressful reality, but one that prevents many headaches later on.

Now that things were well underway with more and more of our first building coming together, I was hit with the reality of just what it was that God was calling us to do. I wrote down a couple of soul-searching prayers in my journal:

December 22, 2007:

Lord, as I get to thinking about accepting children into Gateway, I realize more and more the magnitude of responsibility which is before us in rearing the children and teaching them Your Book and most importantly, about You and how they can have a right relationship with You. Lord, I pray also for our staff – that You would help us to train and disciple them so that they may be strong in You and living examples of Christ in caring for, teaching and discipling the children. Lord, You know every one of the people who will work with us and for us. And You know every child. I commit them all to <u>You</u> and also commit myself to You – for You are the Center and

I desire that You will be the Center of all aspects and facets of Gateway and our lives!

January 11, 2008:

Lord, how will I raise our children – at Gateway and also our own, by Your blessing? Where do we start? How do we start? Am I able? Am I a good role model? Am I a good reflection of You? Am I (is my life) transparent to who You are? Am I fogged over, smoked over? Lord, I feel so incapable, so unable, so useless. …Show me how, dear Lord. How can I glorify Your name in this role?

We spent much time preparing mentally and practically for our first house. We may have been a little too "blue-sky" thinking in some of our purchases (i.e. the four sets of three-tiered bunkbeds wide enough to sleep two kids on each tier). We started searching for our initial staff, someone who would help us to navigate things in the community and eventually help to cook for our initial children we would receive. We approached a lady we were acquainted with from attending the same Khmer church in Phnom Penh. She seemed eager to work with us and was willing to join us in the province. And while Taka camped out at the property the last part of February and into March, I finalized our staff agreement. By the second week of March, she and I made the move to the province. Within the first month of our living there, a team from a church in Japan – introduced to us by former seminary classmates who had been sent as missionaries there – came and blessed us by planting over 30 mango trees on our 1-hectare property.

Within a week of their visit, we officially opened our doors as an orphanage and called it 'Gateway' (in part as a tribute to our 'home' church, Gateway Christian Fellowship, in Canada). About a week before our official opening, we received a pair of sisters, but when they went to their sister's home to spend the Khmer New Year a month later, they refused to return. Even though we had a written contract, we soon found out that blood trumps paper every time. And so, we were without children again.

"Let your light shine before men in such a way that they may see your good works, and glorify your Father who is in heaven." -Matthew 5:16

"He must increase, but I must decrease."

-John 3:30

Chapter 10

Gateway Opens:
The First Two Years: 2008-2010

*I*nitially, when we opened Gateway, we had a low concrete wall with barbed wire and chain-linked fencing around the border of our property. However, there was no gate. We thought the image was beautiful: Gateway without a gate...implying the acceptance of all who enter. However, it wasn't long before we saw the importance of having an actual gate ("all are accepted" was not intended to be extended to cows!) and we contracted to have an iron gate made and fitted to the gaping opening in our fence.

In the meantime, we had a hired hand who helped with odd jobs, from watering the mango and papaya trees to helping find local workers to fix things here and there. It was our caretaker who took the matter of our "childless" state to the village leader. Through this, we began to see that orphans may not be so prevalent and that there was a larger community of poverty-stricken homes with children suffering from lack of nutrition as well as lack of education. We were proffered to consider changing our parameters for accepting children. Our initial reaction was to say no because we did not believe in separating children from their parents, if at all possible. However, we could not offer any solution to help such cases.

Not to be idle, we got involved in the local church down the street and started free English classes for the children and youth in the community. In large part, owing to the fact that one of us was a white person teaching free English classes, we had to get creative with scheduling classes to accommodate the more than 200 kids who were clamoring for a spot in a rather small and limited classroom area. However, as it turned out, after the initial wonder of our classes, more than half would stop coming for one reason or another. Along with our English class initiative, we held youth meetings with a message, meal, and fun and games on Sunday afternoons. We had a great response from the youth during this time and this part of our work carried on for nearly a year.

During this "childless" time, we experienced much doubt: doubt about what we were doing there, why we didn't have any kids, etc. We were also discouraged to hear that though there seemed to be orphans, relatives, no matter how poor they were, were determined to keep the children with them. On the one hand, we understood this connection, the strength of relationship here and filial piety, but at the same time, we were somewhat appalled that the adults would willingly subject children to poverty, malnutrition, and ignorance, when there was a viable option for nutritious food and assured opportunity to go to school by having the children come to live at Gateway.

Finally, Taka was invited to a commune meeting, and the secretary came to our place and listened to us as we explained who we were and what we envisioned to do at Gateway. This was the beginning of a *huge* blessing for us as this man began advising us and vetting the children whom we would get to know about. He also agreed to help with the search, as he had a better knowledge of the needs of the community, and he began leading us to consider children for acceptance into Gateway.

It was at the end of August that we would receive our next children, including a half-blind widow and her young daughter. In those days, the rules and regulations for orphanages were rather lax, and we also learned that not all orphans were disadvantaged and, likewise, not all disadvantaged were orphans. There were numerous poor families – whether having either one or both parents – so we adjusted our criterion for whom God would bring to us to care for. Through a great relationship with the Commune Secretary and through word of mouth, we began receiving more children. By the end of 2008, we had twelve children.

In November, I received a phone call from an expat[10] caregiver of a little girl with HIV. She had an emergency and couldn't find anyone to take the little girl. I quickly agreed, though I did check with Taka, and made arrangements to go to Phnom Penh to pick her up. She was so tiny for someone who was supposedly over a year old. At first, our care for her was to be for six weeks, but in the midst of my reporting her health and well-being to her caregiver (who had left Cambodia for her home country), she made the decision to let us keep her. We made it official by asking the girl's grandmother to come and sign the paperwork and contract to legally receive little Srey Lin into our home.

---

[10] Expat – is a person who lives outside of their native country

With kids now living under our roof, we had to consider the possibility of hiring more staff. We had seen many models of child-care facilities where they hired housemothers to care for a small number of children. Following this model, we began the search to add at least one housemother to the growing family of Gateway. We were already experiencing some conflict with our initial helper and cook; problems with her asserting authority and threatening the children, were among some of the clashes that we had with her. Still, we tried.

There was also the matter of funds. We didn't believe that God had called us without meaning to provide for us. We knew the reality that the more we added to our number meant an increase in expenses. However, we were not to be dismayed or lacking, for God stirred the hearts of people we knew, and many we did not, to offer to become sponsors for individual children. This led us to the sponsorship program where a family sponsors a child monthly and we send quarterly updates with pictures of their child and encouraged exchanging letters from both sides. And God took things a step further: He raised up sponsors beyond the number of children we had. He shook us to our cores to fully feel the effect of his faithfulness to meet our needs even before we knew we had them!

Becoming parents of multiple children without having a background or much of any training in child-rearing had its challenges for us. Everyday there was something new to address, as well as something "old" that had been addressed before. We both experienced the mental and emotional exhaustion of teaching children to follow rules and to understand boundaries – concepts totally foreign to them but were ingrained in our Western upbringings.

On this topic of repeating rules, one of the rules of Gateway was that no one is to hit or kick or use any physical action to cause another pain. One day the youngest sister of one sister trio was tattled on to have hit someone at the school. When we confronted her, she said, "But I didn't do it here. I hit the kid at the school, so it's alright." Obviously, transferrable concepts and critical thinking are not something that is taught. It just floored us how direct and detailed all our rules and teachings would have to be: changing the rules to be all-inclusive: "no hitting anyone anywhere-ever."

My parents came for a visit over Christmas. It was their first-ever visit to Asia. They lavished us with gifts and comforts from the US and helped with the day-to-day menial tasks (like picking lice eggs out of our newest children). They also built a beautiful flowerbed for us to have some greenery and beauty in our court-yard. Their visit overlapped with Taka's parents' arrival for their visit in January. Another team from the church in Japan helped to escort them to Cambodia and Taka made plans to return with them. This was their first-ever trip outside of Japan, so it was a big deal and we were so blessed!

During this visit, we discovered that we had E.coli in our well and my parents helped to fund the digging of a new one. We also had a meeting with our contractor to discuss our options for adding a new semi-detached building to house our growing number of girls. This, along with adding new toilets had a hefty price tag and we told him that we would call him for this new building project once we secured the funds. When my parents returned to the States, they began wading through their mountain of mail and found several envelopes containing more than enough for the new building project in monetary gifts for our ministry; one donor had sent the exact funds that were quoted us by our contractor. This, in and of itself, was a profound and solidifying testament to God's faithful-ness and a concrete affirmation to our feeble hearts and minds that we were indeed living according to the vision that He so graciously entrusted to us.

When I was returning to the province after seeing Taka and his parents off, and later my parents off, I got a call from our cook. She was wondering when I would get back because she was quitting her job and the motorcycle taxi was waiting at our gate. I'll admit, this hit me like a ton of bricks. Yes, we had been having issues with her for some time, but I wasn't expecting her to quit on us. Thankfully, we had a gardener on the premises who agreed to step in and take over cooking until we could find and hire someone new.

This first year and a half of Gateway was full of trials. At first, we thought we would follow the pattern of some existing children centers. Following the model of hiring housemothers was a seemingly good way of caring for a large number of children, placing housemothers over the charge of 5-10 children. However, over the course of twelve months, we hired and fired fourteen women for several reasons: dishonesty, not following our methods for disciplining the children, hitting and threatening the children, and running up tabs in the market while pocketing the cash we entrusted to them to buy groceries. After all that heartache and headache, we finally concluded, for our own peace of mind and for the safety of our children, that Taka and I would evermore be the acting parents and disciplinarians and only hire a woman to cook meals and be an extra adult figure on the property.

There were times of feeling utterly overwhelmed, but then God would open my eyes to see each of our children as He did. Though tiresome, quarrelsome and naughty, each one radiated God's image and His love for them would fill my heart. He assured us through their innocent faces, just how blessed we were to be entrusted with the care for these precious ones.

Sadly, some children could not cope with the seemingly restrictive environment of Gateway. When coming from a home with loose boundaries and no set rules and entering a place that has clear boundaries and rules took some getting used to. Whenever we took in new children, we had to learn to keep the first few months as a trial run to see whether or not they could integrate. Having this mindset eased some of the heartache of children coming and going—some in a matter of days. After one such departure, I journaled about my feelings of failure:

March 31, 2009:

Lord, we had another one leave us yesterday...we went through [all the benefits of staying versus the life of poverty] and even with the kids trying to persuade her to change her mind, still she wanted to go home. And so she went. Lord, this is so disconcerting! Altogether 5 children have come and chosen to leave us of their own mind. What does this mean? How can we avoid such an experience in the future? Lord, we give this to You. You are our Lord, our Shepherd. Guide us in Your wisdom, Lord.

2009 also saw our first trip to the beach with our first eight children (some children had already left us for various reasons). We also had our first baptismal service where three were baptized. Four of the children had been actively pursuing a new faith in God over the previous months of their time with us at Gateway, but the fourth had an ear infection, preventing her from being baptized that trip.

Our second summer in the province, we were extremely blessed to receive our first-ever short-term volunteer, a Japanese lady currently living in the US. She had found us through an on-line search and contacted us by email. She came for two months and filled her time with holding first aid, hygiene, and other classes and lessons. Though her time with us was brief, we were very much encouraged by her and through her.

The end of her stay, we were finally able to begin the building of our second, semi-detached building to accommodate the growing number of girls. The initial living arrangements were in one building with Taka, Lin and me living on the top level and all the children living in the ground floor, comprised of two large bedrooms and two bathrooms. As more and more girls were added, we decided that we needed, not only more rooms, but to separate the boys from the girls. This new building had two new bedrooms and an open walkway with iron gates to lock in place for safety reasons. We also added 3 new bathrooms. Along with this new building, we had a rooftop that provided a nice pavilion once we completed it with railings and a roof.

During the latter part of 2009, we also saw spiritual growth and awakening in our children with new professions of faith and witnessing their hunger for more of God. This was constantly challenged at the public school where the kids went to study: especially with the rampant corruption that seems ingrained in Cambodian society. By this time, we had begun a morning ritual of sending them off to school with prayer and a few praise songs to help them face the challenges at the school they attended. We prayed fervently for spiritual protection over our kids' hearts and also for wisdom and discernment for how to continue to lead and guide them day-to-day. We added two Bible study meetings to our week: one on Sunday and another mid-week. And we were blessed to see them begin approaching Taka with more questions from what we were teaching and what they were reading for themselves and how to live it out.

Another aspect to our life is the fact that we also wanted to start adding to our Miyano family. By late 2009, we had been trying for a baby of our own for over a year. I struggled and prayed over this aspect of our lives – yearning for a child, yet also learning to hand over this desire to God's hands and His timing. We had a full life and were still navigating the waters: learning as we went, for we had no practical training for this at all.

We also had to come to grips with what was available in terms of health care. The village afforded very minimal care, so we would make trips to Phnom Penh for any major concerns. Some of the health issues that came up included an outbreak of the Chickenpox (of which Taka had never been exposed to and ended up quarantining himself in Phnom Penh through the worst of it). In retrospect, we can only stand amazed at how God protected everyone in our care whenever one of us needed to travel to the city, leaving the other to oversee our growing family. If there had been an emergency of any kind, I do not know what we would have done! God is so good to us. We never had any incident of thieves or an outbreak of any illness (aside from the very manageable chickenpox) or severe accident whatsoever. It could only have been God's hand of grace over us throughout that time.

In early 2010, I made a trip to Phnom Penh to check mail, receive some funds and have an overnight reprieve. After my return, I was unable to find my passport and naturally I thought I had lost it, or it had been stolen. This led me to filing a police report and requesting a new passport. While it was being processed, we found my passport that had been "hidden" by Srey Lin. Since I couldn't cancel my new passport, it meant that I would have to take a trip out of the country for my visa. So, I contacted a rather abstract relative (my dad's cousin's son had married a Thai girl and she was visiting her family in Bangkok) and I spent a week with her and her family.

Chapter 11

Miyano Family Growth

*U*pon my return from Bangkok, I was delighted to discover that I was pregnant. When we first broached the subject of having a baby, Taka's initial response was to send me back to America. When I began asking the expat community for their opinions, most seemed to either travel to their home countries or go to Thailand. Cambodia simply does not have any NICU facility. With that in mind, I found a new hospital in Phnom Penh that was in partnership with an international hospital in Bangkok (so that if one needed more desperate measures, a patient would be medevac'd to that hospital). At the time, they even had a Japanese OB-GYN on staff, and I began seeing her for monthly check-ups.

In April, we took the kids to the beach for a second time. Taka and I had taken an advanced trip to secure affordable accommodations and to make connections with a local restaurant to cater to the needs of our large group of twenty-five kids. Upon our return, we ran into some rather unpleasant roadblocks with our staff. At the time we had two and neither one was fulfilling her required tasks to the level that we had taught and asked of them. In the end, we decided on dismissal. This led to the discovery that both women had run tabs at the market with our food vendors (we would give the necessary funds for groceries, they would pocket the funds, and after their departure, the vendors came knocking).

This led to the institution of new regulations: we met with the vendors we frequented and set up a ledger account with each one individually. We instructed our helpers and staff to use only those vendors and we spread the word among all the vendors to not lend to any staff of Gateway, forewarning that we would not take any responsibility.

With the growing number of kids and our tiny dining area not meeting the required space, we decided to upgrade one area of our compound and made it into a canteen. This was completed around the same time as our pavilioned rooftop mentioned earlier. Also, due to the extension of our family with a new baby on the way, we decided to update our upstairs living apartment with outfitting our second room into a nursery, which included the purchase and installment of a wall air conditioning unit. We also installed our first washing machine.

Due to these latter renovations, I took Lin with me to Phnom Penh where we stayed for six weeks until the renovations were complete. We were blessed to be offered the spare room of a friend in town for most of our stay. Also, with these added renovations, we encountered some financial strain, causing us to borrow funds from Taka's parents that would eventually be paid back as Gateway received extra funds here and there over the next few years.

About the time of the start of all these renovations, Taka and I came to the realization that there were many things in our ministry and life that weren't really working cohesively. I journaled in more detail what we were experiencing around that time:

May 11, 2010:

Lord, as You know, for some time both Taka and I have felt like we are stuck in some kind of spiritual peat bog – so many things around us, but no clear direction – yet if we stop moving other things will bog us down, sucking at our feet until we can't move any direction.

Lord, that is what we are praying for – <u>direction</u>! Where do we go from here; how do we get out; how do we get to where You want us to go?

On the one hand it is good to be in this situation for we cry out to You for help and we can see where we are and see our areas of individual, as well as ministry, needs. You know how we are – always wanting to be moving forward with a plan towards a goal… but right now we are lacking something to look forward to, to grasp onto – to strive for. And then a part of me thinks, "Do we really <u>need</u> to have a plan?" Not necessarily, but some direction would be nice so that we can focus our efforts and prayers to that.

In spite of the undercurrent angst we were feeling, we were still unsure what we were to do differently and continued to pray for the Lord's leading. We continued to teach and to lead worship. We played with the children and worked on building lasting relationships with each of the children. We helped to cultivate one boy's penchant for drawing by challenging him to look past the strict and rigid forms of artwork that he knew from class and to strike out to draw what he saw. He took the challenge and presented us with new creations very often.

Taka decided to learn how to play the guitar, which also encouraged some of our children to learn as well. We made a small booklet of Christian songs in Khmer to sing together (compiled from a couple of Khmer songbooks). And I even began to translate a couple of other songs into Khmer to teach the children as well.

We worked side-by-side with the children doing chores together, making crafts together and encouraging self-review of classwork. We openly praised children for good progress reports and encouraged those who were lagging behind.

One particular instance still stands out in my mind when one of the girls came to Taka and proudly presented herself to him. When he asked her what she was so happy about, she lifted her school skirt to reveal several scrawled writings on her thigh. On further investigation, we found that she had used her notes while taking a test. The innocent pride she had in this crafty way of cheating led us to start teaching more fervently the truth and how it pertains to daily life. Cheating and lying is not acceptable in God's eyes— even if everyone is doing it. And letting others to peek off your test is also a form of cheating.

In the midst of all this, we still looked ahead to our new addition. By this time, we had found out that we were having a girl. Taka insisted on knowing the gender so that we could nail down a name as soon as possible. We decided to give her a Japanese name, incorporating the Chinese symbol, or Kanji, for "holy". After striking out with some of the options, Taka finally found the name we would call her: Senoka (聖乃香). Her name means "aroma of holiness."

As I entered my final month of pregnancy, we heard for the first time of the new shift in the government concerning care for children within the Kingdom. I captured my initial reaction to this information in my journal:

October 14, 2010:

We heard from [our pastor friend] that the government of Cambodia is looking to streamline the care of orphans back into a more nuclear family structure → a structure which no longer calls for nor needs orphanages. <u>So</u> ... it means that we may have to "recalibrate" our vision if the government does not [consider our umbrella NGO's] orphanage to be such that warrants a continuation of permission to work with orphans...[This] brings a kind of unsettling side to our thinking and even future planning. What else could we do here? What would happen to our kids? Would we have to send them back to their relatives'? Could we somehow have a "back-up" plan which would enable us to stay here and the children as well while we "re-vamped" and re-directed our focus? ...

Lord, <u>all</u> things are in Your hands. Help us to wait on You, knowing that You will guide us [constantly] continually. Help us to trust You, Lord. You know that neither one of us is particularly thrilled with the idea that we may need to go back to Japan or the States. What would we do there? Would we simply find jobs and live out our lives in a capacity such as that? I know that if You did lead us there that we would strive to be used as Your beacons and instruments of truth – but honestly I (and I know Taka as well) am not too excited with that prospect... However, I will go withersoever You lead me, Lord. Give me the strength to let go of <u>my</u> ideas and to follow You with all abandon.

However, though this initial indication was given, it would be several more years before we could finally see the fruits of this declaration of a shift in the care for children.

About 3 weeks before my due date (initially due November 5th, but bumped back to November 3rd), I moved to a hotel to be close to the hospital, just in case Senoka tried to make an early appearance

(Taka had a great fear of me going into labor in the province and not being able to get to the hospital on time). My parents were scheduled to arrive late on October 31ˢᵗ. Just a few days after I relocated, Taka called me in the middle of the night to ask me to call one of our commune's policemen and request their presence at Gateway. Without any explanation at the time, imagine just how panicked I felt being so far away and worried for Taka and Lin and for all the kids at Gateway. I finally found out that Taka caught two men in masks on our balcony trying to break in. This security breech prompted Taka to contact our contractor to put in extra security measures: essentially turning our property into a caged-in, yet safe, inner compound to keep any intruders out.

A couple of days after my parents arrived, the would-be thieves made a second attempt of breaking in (before our contractor could begin work), and Taka brought Lin to Phnom Penh out of concern for her safety and also due to her having a high fever. It was November 3ʳᵈ.

In the wee hours of November 4ᵗʰ, I awoke to check Lin's fever and also due to pangs I associated with diarrhea. When all attempts to use the toilet proved fruitless, I started timing the waves of pain. Sure enough, they were regular, and we all trooped to the hospital just after 7am. I called Taka but told him I would let him know if he should try to make it to Phnom Penh or not. (The direct bus leaves by 7am, but he could take a motorcycle taxi to the main highway to flag down a commercial bus or minivan). I was admitted at 8:30 after confirming that I was indeed in labor. I was grateful for my doctor who safe-guarded my requests for what I wanted and didn't want for my birth plan. I contacted Taka to tell him that Senoka was on her way, but it was really too late for him to catch a bus to get there in time for her birth.

While Grandpa (my dad) took care of Lin, Grandma (my mom) accompanied me to the delivery room where I sat in a chair and dozed between contractions (which was quite a feat since contractions were less than 5 minutes apart at this time). When it was finally coming to the homestretch, I was told to get on the delivery bed. The nurses all around me were Thai—so I couldn't even attempt a conversation. They would be talking away together and when they noticed I was having a contraction, would clasp fingertips and start to do a high-pitched humming sound. It wasn't exactly soothing or uplifting, if you ask me! Finally, my doctor came in and told me that it was time to push. On the first push, my water broke. And then, after only a few more pushes, Senoka arrived just after 11:35. I had never been so happy. About that time, Lin had awakened from her nap and wanted Mama. My mom got her from the waiting room and brought her to me. We went to the room I was to stay for the next two nights after some repair was done for tearing during birth. Taka came the next day to meet Senoka, stayed for lunch, and then took Lin back to Gateway.

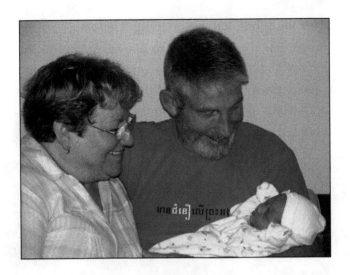

After my initial 2-day hospitalization (as per the birth package I had opted for at the hospital), we ended up staying in the hotel for a week and then we made the bus ride back to Bos Khnor when Seno was 10 days old. I must say, having a baby out in public went against many social norms in Cambodia and I was sometimes accosted by the vendors and any number of bystanders to find out Senoka's gender and given all manner of advice for how to hold her and feed her properly.

However, our initial stay in the province was short-lived since renovations were not yet complete and there was a plethora of dust shrouding our little compound. The main part of the work that was left was to replace our false ceiling with sheet metal. This prompted me to make a trip with Senoka and my parents to the beach. When the renovations were finally completed, we returned to the province and enjoyed the rest of my parents' stay until just before Taka's and my fifth anniversary.

December 12, 2010:

Lord, please give us specific guidance regarding Gateway: its children, its future as a church, ways to serve the community, everything. There are so many things that we would like to do but getting to the point of actually 'doing' hasn't arrived yet. We don't want Gateway to be powered by us – for this is Your work. Help us to keep <u>You</u> at the forefront of everything – for it is <u>all</u> about You – <u>You</u> are the life force.

Chapter 12

The Next 2 Years and a Big Move

*S*hortly after the New Year 2011, we had another team from Japan come and visit. Again, they brought Taka's parents for their second visit, largely to meet their newest grandchild, Senoka. This visit, however brief, was an added blessing to our relationship.

When Taka escorted them back to Japan for this trip, we began to feel the separation a bit more keenly. Since the beginning of the work of Gateway, we had been praying for partners in ministry. Until we received such partners – whether reliable Khmer staff or other missionaries, Taka and I could not travel out of Cambodia together. So, when he would travel to Japan, I stayed at Gateway. And when I would travel to the States, likewise, he would stay. It was (and still is to this day) a precarious situation should any emergency arise, but by His grace, we have never encountered anything of the kind. But having a new baby and upwards of twenty other children besides, left us a bit more on edge. It also kept us in a state where we constantly kept Christ in the forefront of our days and nights through prayer.

Life kept moving forward and we needed to work out the ever-increasing dynamics of living together with 20+ kids. We had to deal with rivalry among the children, usually spear-headed by two of the oldest girls who would then gather their "troops" among the rest of the kids until there was a definitive line of whose side a child was on. And since we couldn't always catch the under-current until the riptide pulled our feet out from under us, we had to do a lot of counseling to dig down to the catalyst that started it all—sometimes dating back to months before and usually over something that was pithy and relatively minor.

We had to do a lot of "basic training" with anger management and problem solving, including conflict-resolution. It seemed that the kids would simply harbor the perceived slights against them until they couldn't handle the load and would "explode" over everyone in the house. We did our best to meet together to calmly hear both sides of the stories brought to our attention, but most of the time, admittedly, Taka and I would get to the point of exac-erbation and simply punish both parties in some way and make pointed efforts to add Biblical teaching on grace and serving one another and love.

Proximity to about half our children's extended relations was also an increasing issue. Since they were so close, it was quite common for some of the children to take liberties and divert their routes to or from school to pay a short visit to them. When we first caught wind of this, we had to meet with the relatives in question and openly forbid the children such visits as it was deemed unfair to the other children, not to mention undermining our authority. Every child had opportunities to travel to their relatives' homes over the two major holidays in the year: April for the Khmer New Year, and over their summer holiday, either in August or September. It took us several years of frustrating schedule differences to lay down the rule that all children would leave over a certain set time so that we didn't get left with wondering "Who is going next?" or "When is so-and-so returning?" Like I said, much of the formation for our work was learned and perfected through trial and error while we learned as time moved forward.

Gateway was maintaining quite well, in outside appearance. We had many issues among the children, including, but not limited to jealousy, rivalry, rebellion, etc., and, of course, the ever-present staffing issues. But we were not at peace. We had envisioned doing so much more with our large property in the province: but all those aspiring projects were contingent on partners working together with us. Essentially, we were treading water. Taka had reached a stagnant place emotionally and spiritually in the work we were doing at Gateway. Like me, he was struggling with the "sameness" of his day-to-day activities of caring for the kids. He found great joy and encouragement in teaching God's Word to them, but there was still the yearning to do more...

In the summer of 2011, I took Senoka for her first visit to the US to have a chance to share her with some of my older relations. She met my Grandpa Fred and some of her great aunts and uncles. This would be the last time that I would see my Grandpa Fred, and I cherish the memories that I was able to have with him while we reminisced between the four generations within our family. This same summer, I also took an opportunity to take a short road trip to Canada to visit our church home of Gateway in Regina. It had been more than five years since we had been commissioned by them and it was a blessing to touch base with our many supporters and spiritual mentors during a long weekend stay. Since we bookended our trip with short stays in Japan with Taka's parents, I also took an opportunity to visit and share at one of our supporting churches in Tokyo.

With Lin staying in Cambodia, we began to research what it would take for us to be able to include Lin in these trips. And though international adoptions were closed at that point for Cambodia, we began pursuing what legal rights we could have to Lin so that we could travel outside of Cambodia with her. Her current status of being under the guardianship of Gateway didn't do much by way of rights to travel with her, etc. So, we contacted a lawyer to request assistance in gaining legal guardianship of her. We kept all things candid with Lin's birth grandma, who supported us in our endeavors to care for Lin as our own daughter. However, due to the lengthy process, we wouldn't receive a court certificate authorizing us as foster parents until Senoka was nearly a year old. It would take a total of fifteen months beyond that before we had her passport in hand and an official permission from the Ministry to travel outside of Cambodia with her.

Back in Cambodia, we started a new round of renovations to help ensure better security of our inner compound, as well as ensure our water source. The one well we used on the property fed our house through an electric pump filling a 1,000L tank. However, when prolonged power cuts occurred, we would then run out of water. So, we added a new pump well with a pumping tower that was hooked up to gravity-fed tubing that ran to fill a couple of water reservoirs. We also added a much larger water tank that would also have a pipe to fill the holding vases to ensure a presence of water for Gateway in any condition.

Around the time of Senoka's first birthday, my physical health started having issues. Senoka was also affected with a prolonged cough and we both took trips every two weeks to Phnom Penh for follow-up care for upper respiratory problems and persistent coughs that would last more than three months.

Even with a prescribed inhaler, I still experienced very scary episodes where I would not be able to get any air in or out. I would sit there straining to take a breath with tears streaming down my face. After the second of such episodes, Taka and I had a very serious talk about our future in the province. With my having to travel to Phnom Penh so often without any known cause for my health issues, coupled with the growing realization that there were simply no opportunities to broaden our children's horizons while living in the province, we began to consider and converse on the topic of uprooting Gateway and moving everyone to Phnom Penh.

Phnom Penh is a growing city and with a city comes much more in the way of opportunities and helping to facilitate the potential of any one of our children. The decision to move was a bit surprising after having lived in the province for nearly four years and having poured so much into our property. There was no lack for our children because we would take them all with us.

In January 2012, we made a firm commitment to start the process for researching houses in Phnom Penh. It meant searching on-line real estate sites and Taka making some trips to Phnom Penh to do some groundwork by driving through possible communities that have easy access to schools and markets. Through a real estate agent, Taka viewed several properties for consideration, but essentially, none met our desires for Gateway: either too small, too expensive or just too far from anything we needed. By God's grace, Taka chanced to drive by a townhouse for rent after making a wrong turn. It was this house that ended up being *the one* for Gateway.

On the flipside of us finding a property in Phnom Penh, there was the issue of what to do with our property in the province. Humanly speaking, it was our desire to close on the sale of our property and then turn around and use the funds to buy a property in Phnom Penh. However, the realist in Taka pushed us forward with approaching both our parents to loan us the cash needed to buy the property in Phnom Penh first, with the idea that we would repay them upon the completion of the sale of our property in the province.

We started reaching out to those in our network of contacts living in Cambodia, or who also had contacts living in the country, who might have an interest in purchasing our property for future ministry work. It was our deepest desire that our property would be continued as a legacy of God's Light in the community. However, even after a wider net had been cast with social media and other advertising, we would make the move without so much as a "nibble" or reasonable counteroffer to what we were asking for the property.

With the sale finalized the end of March, we commenced to the minor renovations we needed to make the "Pteah L'veng" (Khmer for what is most comparable to a townhouse or row house in the US) more suitable to accommodate our family needs and Gateway needs. Most of the renovations were centered on making our Miyano living quarters more private as well as adding on 3 more bathrooms to help with the capacity of our children.

Lin, Senoka and I moved into the house with the first load of furnishings the beginning of July. We started setting up house and getting to know the area so that we could have our bearings about us when everyone made the final move on August 6th. I began searching for and vetting options for hiring a new house helper for Gateway, namely, a cook. Through our connections, we were reintroduced to a lady we have known since our first year in Phnom

Penh. She helped us to arrange home deliveries of all our groceries with orders made by phone and money passing from us directly to the vendors.

During this last month of living in the province, Gateway was experiencing some financial issues when the cash boxes came to be nearly $200 short. Though we couldn't pinpoint any one person who would break into our living quarters to steal the money, it was still disconcerting, to say the least.

It wasn't until after we moved to Phnom Penh that the culprit struck again, and we finally caught him red-handed. It was one of the newest boys to Gateway. When we searched his person, we found that he had also swiped our digital camera from our family apartment. The feeling of being violated and repeatedly duped was an especially huge blow to Taka and me. We contacted his mother and Taka ended up taking the boy back to the province to hand him over to her, as well as hold a meeting with the local police for his indiscretion. However, because the theft occurred on our property, the local authorities did not feel it was their jurisdiction and offered us no recourse or restitution other than that we would leave him with his mother.

Chapter 13

A New Place, New Opportunities

*O*ne of the possible hopes in moving to the city was to consider options for sending Lin and Senoka to an accredited international school. However, upon further research, we found that it was simply impossible to consider spending the nearly $10,000/ year it would cost for both of them to attend either of the Christian schools with the lowest tuition fees. Thus, I continued my homeschooling teaching career.

Through some interesting connections, Taka was introduced to a Japanese pastor who asked about the possibility of our accepting a fresh seminary graduate to work as an intern with us for 3 months as part of her formational training. This would be our first intern and we welcomed her with open hearts.

I was also struggling at the time with a great spiritual drought. I began looking for a community of women where I would have space to learn and grow in faith. In September I began attending an international ladies' Bible Study and it was the lifeline I needed to keep me on solid ground of faith. It was through this group that my bearings were realigned, and I began to thrive again in my faith and in my roles as mom, homeschool teacher and in the work of Gateway.

As the kids began school in Phnom Penh, we found that there was a steep learning curve from where they had been in the province. This was especially apparent with our 7th graders who had a lot of ground to make up, especially regarding their English language abilities. Even though the school has a set curriculum to follow for teaching English, there are many gaps that need to be filled – mostly by taking classes at other schools.

For some, the struggle was very great. In fact, one of the oldest girls decided to run away. She had asked permission to meet her Grandpa at the bus depot that goes directly to the province, but when she didn't return, we found out from the other kids that she had intended to run away. We called her mother and informed her to be expecting her and, though we knew the consequences of her actions, had to release her from Gateway.

In November of 2012, we finally received Lin's passport and we began the lengthy process of applying for a permit to take her overseas. We learned through this process that we needed to give an extended grace period for our projected travel dates as sometimes the amount of time for a document to pass through all the

proper channels can take weeks. This ignorance on our part forced
a delay in travel. Finally, in March of 2013, Lin went with Taka to
Japan to visit his family.

As was mentioned earlier, we had a widow living with us together
with her daughter since the very early days of Gateway. Early in
2013, she was offered an opportunity for autonomy by living on
a relative's property in the province. Though we dissuaded her in
lieu of her daughter's education (in a country with "free" public
schools, it is actually quite expensive for single-parent families),
she still chose to leave us. We began praying for another live-in
staff and God answered in a way that we were not expecting. An
acquaintance of ours had met a lady from India who was searching
for a way that she could serve Cambodian children. After meeting
with her and learning her desires and heart to serve, we came to an
understanding for providing food, lodging and a meager stipend
and she came to live with us for nearly two years from March 2013.
Throughout her time at Gateway, she enjoyed teaching the children
English, Bible and songs. Her years of experience as a pastor in
children's ministries was an added blessing to our Gateway kids.

As the first year of living in Phnom Penh was coming to an end, we were constantly on the lookout for opportunities for our children. Some opportunities were considered and dismissed; such as the possibility of sending them to a private school with many more electives. However, after prayerful and consideration, it proved to not be in our kids' best interest, nor within the capacity of our monthly budget.

In April, when all the kids had left for the provinces, we had a surprise visit from Srey Lin's biological mother. This was the second time we had met her (her first visit came shortly after we had first moved to Phnom Penh when she came with Lin's Grandmother). She did not look to be in good health and was in town to receive her medication for HIV. We had a hard time gauging just how her visit affected Lin. She couldn't really communicate since her first language is English and her mother doesn't know any. We had to answer many questions from Lin as curiosity about her birth mom came and went with these intermittent visits that usually ended with her asking for money for one thing or another.

With the number of kids in our care, we decided that we needed to add something to our home to help us take them around. This led us to ordering our own tuk-tuk to be made (essentially, a built-in motorcycle to an extended trailer with benches down the sides) and Taka learned how to drive it. Though there always seemed to be some glitch here and there, especially when it rained, this tuk-tuk served us rather well over the course of four years. This helped to cut down on costs in terms of hiring other tuk-tuks whenever we wanted to go somewhere with a group of kids.

In the first year we were in Phnom Penh, we had several kinds of visitors, staying anywhere from just an afternoon to several months. Sometimes we struggled with what to "provide" for such visitors as many come with the unspoken request for us to provide an activity or project for them to join or facilitate. As we muddled through some visitors, we finally concluded that since we don't have special projects, anyone desiring to come and bless us with their presence should do so within their own unique gifting and calling. Sometimes we had to delve into the reality that some ideas were more aspirational than realistic. Some things just can't translate in this culture and some needed items are not readily available.

Some of our visitors incited new rules and regulations, more for our sanity and emotional well-being, but also for the safety of the visitors and for our children. We had to draw a line about loaning money when on several occasions, a guest ran into a financial difficulty (ATM cards frozen, etc). It was difficult to muddle through without any standards, but each incident gave us greater wisdom for the next situation. These new rules induced us to have regulations printed up for any future visitors and we strongly encouraged new visitors to refer to our rules and also had an initial briefing session with new visitors to further explain the reasons behind such rules.

Over the summer holiday, I heard about a Community Dance Workshop geared toward children living in care. I contacted the instructor and this workshop turned into an invaluable partnership of dance. Several of our girls joined the two-day workshop. At the end of the month, the instructor asked if four of our girls would like to continue and do a dance project to perform at the school's end-of-the-year dance performance. This even spilled over into the New Year when they joined a short dance film to be made for the Arts Film Festival later in January. On the tails of this dance film, the instructor went out of his way to find a sponsor for one of our girls to start taking ballet at the school. She started in the spring of 2014 with private classes to get her up to speed with other dancers her age and to help her integrate with language and ballet terms. This started a journey that I will share more on later.

Since the school was first and foremost a ballet school, we decided to enroll Lin in her first ballet class when she was six. She took to it with gusto and we enjoyed watching her. Senoka mimicked Lin while watching from the outside until she was able to join when they opened another class for younger students when she was five. They enjoyed learning dance over the following five or so years, increasing their abilities and taking part in the various group recitals, as well as solos.

For our Gateway girls, over the next several years, they would be involved in various levels of dance training and projects. The community dance group performed five other times that included children and youth from other organizations. As time went on, our girls were challenged in new roles as mentors of the younger dancers and also to help in choreographing segments of the dances that they were to perform.

Another aspect was something that the studio called the "youth development dance track" where they were invited to have a more rounded formation of dance in joining the adult ballet and contemporary classes. Later on, several of them joined the youth company, a small group of dancers where they choreographed and performed beautiful pieces together with other international students. They were also given opportunities to learn the discipline of teaching small children movement and dance. Another partnership borne out of this was to learn theology behind their beliefs and learn how to tell Bible stories through movement and dance. This project was then shared at two centers for children where they brought the gospel through the medium of dance. Dance has given these girls an avenue for expression in a way that would not be possible verbally. We have seen our girls grow into young women of confidence throughout this whole learning process and have seen their lives enriched from these invaluable experiences that they have been blessed to have.

At Gateway, we also received several new children during this time. Some were relatives of children already in our care, and others came by word of mouth. Not all would make it through the preliminary probationary period and would, therefore, return to their respective relatives who had signed them over to our care. Each time someone left, we constantly had the niggling sense of doubt worrying us about what we were doing wrong that children couldn't come and stay at Gateway. We had many people tell us things that we already knew: "God used you for this short amount of time and only He knows the impact their time at Gateway will have on their future," etc., etc. All that is well and good, but it didn't really lessen the sting of each departure—especially when it was a child who had been with us for some time, like the girl who ran away after having been with us for five years.

Having a live-in volunteer also warranted new regulations and standards. Initially, we had to learn how to interact with each other and help her to find her niche within Gateway. As time went on, we started teaching her and explaining to her the reasons for the way we approach issues in certain ways and had to ward off miscommunication as we tried to have a united front as Gateway leadership. In some ways, she was a softy in her approach to discipline, which conflicted with some of the hardline approaches that we had in certain situations. Though our live-in volunteer was mature in age, she still had some difficulty with discernment in other areas, especially in the area of romantic relationships. She had never married but seemed to be seeking for a relationship. She found an outlet in mingling with men on social media. In conversations with her, we warned her about keeping boundaries and taking care in divulging information, etc.

However, in December, she decided to go against our advice and met one of her online contacts. This led to a very unfortunate incident that landed her in the hospital for emergency surgery just a week before she was to depart for the Christmas season in her hometown in India. This really rattled our cages and induced us to take an even firmer stance on the regulations and use of personal devices in our home-especially where our children could see. We had meetings with her and with all the children to warn against the dangers of social media.

During this time, Taka and I began praying for another child and, in the fall of 2013, we were delighted to find that I was pregnant. I returned to the same hospital where Senoka was born but ended up seeing four different doctors for several reasons. I also researched other options for giving birth in Cambodia. But in January, everything changed...

Chapter 14

A New Addition –
With New Challenges

*I*n January, when I went in for my 16-week ultrasound, we not only found out that we were having a boy, but I also noticed that our baby's head had a lot of "empty" space in the cranial cavity. Having a nephew with hydrocephalus, I knew something was wrong. When I consulted the doctor about what I feared, she confirmed it and then blithely told me that I should make plans to either go back to the US or to Thailand and have an abortion.

When I told her that I would keep the baby, she told me straight out that I should not give birth here because there was no follow-up care for such handicapped babies. I remember leaving the doctor's office and joining Taka and the girls at an indoor playground. My first response was that I couldn't have the baby in Cambodia-that I needed to get ready to spend months apart from my family to have our baby in America, where he could get the care he would need. Also, knowing the extent of my nephew's condition, my mind and my heart was freaking out about whether I would be able to cope, able to mother, able to care for him. I was also guilt-ridden, wondering if there had been something that I had done or didn't do that had made this happen to my son.

Taka had already been working on names for our new addition, but he had only been able to come up with one boy name. Still using the Chinese character, or Kanji, for "holy", but with a different pronunciation, we decided to name our son Masato (聖翔): which means "Holy one" (some translations say, "Righteous one") "Soaring." We prayed together for Masato, believing that God was forming him and that we committed him to God's care and design.

I contacted my mom and dad (who had actually moved to the family farm near Springfield, Missouri, after my grandma died) with the news gleaned from the ultrasound and she immediately called the local perinatal clinic to see if they were accepting new patients. When she found out they were, she had them pencil me in for an appointment in February (they couldn't do it sooner because the doctor was actually in Cambodia touring the medical facilities all over the country). So, I booked a flight and arrived for a 10-day-stay. My new doctor administered an amniocentesis and also did an ultrasound. We could see on the more state-of-the-art ultrasound that our son not only had hydrocephalus, but Chiari II malformation and spina bifida (the same three things my nephew has).

A brief pause to explain the terms I just threw out there:

Hydrocephalus is a chronic, neurological condition caused by an abnormal accumulation of cerebrospinal fluid (CSF), resulting in pressure on the brain.[11]

In normal people, this fluid is drained constantly into the spinal column. However, Masato's was not draining properly, and the fluid remained; a condition which, left unchecked, produces pressure against the brain and could cause all manner of disabilities.

Chiari II Malformation is characterized by downward displacement of the medulla, fourth ventricle and cerebellum into the

---

[11] Hydrocephalus Association, "What is Hydrocephalus", https://www. hydroassoc.org/what-is-hydrocephalus -an-overview/ accessed August 20, 2019.

cervical spinal canal, as well as elongation of the pons and fourth ventricle. [12]

What this means is that the cerebellum is usually shaped like a miniature brain at the base of the skull. When it is pulled down, it begins to look more like an ice cream cone and, in severe cases, completely blocks the spinal column preventing normal drainage.

Spina Bifida is when a baby's spine and spinal cord don't develop properly in the womb, causing a gap in the spine.[13]

It is a condition of varying degrees in which the vertebrae have not fully formed and leaves the spinal cord vulnerable. In our son's case, he had the most severe form of the defect with the spinal cord actually outside of the body cavity and concealed in a sac of fluid, referred to as myelomeningocele.

In the midst of all this information, my doctor offered to refer me to a hospital in Texas where a doctor friend of hers was training and overseeing the surgical team in doing inutero repairs of all manner of birth defects, among them spinal repair of babies with myelomeningocele spina bifida.[14] The option of doing this surgery has proven to help the child greatly. With Masato's "lesion" of where his spine is exposed, the level of disability could mean that he would never walk. However, the inutero repair had been proven, in most cases, to reduce the level of disabilities by two vertebrae (as if Masato's wound was two vertebrae smaller than it was)—in Masato's case, it would allow him the use of his knee and hip flexors and give him the possibility of walking.

---

[12] American Association of Neurological Surgeons, "Chiari Malformation", https://www.aans.org/ Patients/Neurosurgical-Conditions-and-Treatments/ Chiari-Malformation, accessed August 20, 2019.

[13] NHS, "Overview: Spina bifida", https://www.nhs.uk/conditions/spina-bifida/ , accessed August 20, 2019.

[14] Texas Children's Hospital, "Spina bifida (Myelomeningocele)" https://women. texaschildrens.org/ program/texas-childrens-fetal-center/conditions-we-treat/ spina-bifida-myelomeningocele , accessed August 20, 2019.

My doctor also told me that I would need to rethink my decision to continue living in Cambodia. This was like a slap in the face—God wasn't saying anything to Taka or me to the effect that He was using this to change our current work and involvement in the life we had at Gateway. But it was words from people like this, and also others speaking out of fear, that began to overwhelm me. I began to fall in line with their thinking and wondered if there was any truth in what was said. I constantly wondered and worried over what my son and his condition would do to change our lives and whether or not his life, care, and needs could be met and sustained in Cambodia, which is a borderline second/third-world country.

I remember a time when I received a particularly unsettling comment, and then getting a call from my brother who was living in Oregon at the time. In the midst of my meltdown, he told me to stop and simply place my hand on my belly and to thank God for the little miracle growing inside of me. This helped to turn me back from the brink of despair and he continued to encourage me with his own journey with his son. That though, humanly speaking, this could potentially be something devastating, that he has been nothing but blessed by his son.

As I finished out this initial visit to the States, I applied for emergency Medicaid to cover costs of the pregnancy and delivery (a 6-month coverage). I flew back to Cambodia to share all I had learned face-to-face with Taka and to talk about what steps we would take as a family. There was also the unspoken stigma that since my brother had a son with spina bifida, that Masato's genes were therefore a condition that came from me. Though I didn't know this line of thinking until much later, it was still an undercurrent reality that several people would attest to when trying to explain the cause for Masato's condition.

With the news of the option of inutero surgery, we decided to move forward. I was tentatively scheduled for an initial diagnostic appointment on March 4th. Taka and I decided to live believing and hoping in God's miraculous healing of Masato-no longer entertaining a moment's thought to the very distressing diagnosis. We decided to live each day supporting and praying for Masato, our miraculous son. So, after two weeks in Cambodia, I made the trip back to the US without any knowledge of how long I would be there.

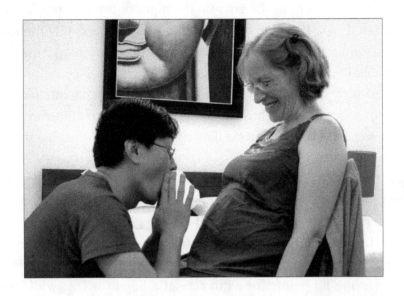

This brief intermission at home was packed with opportunities for me to pour into our girls and to pour into God's Word. Through this time, I received so many blessings and promises to tide me over the next several months. This does not mean that it was not hard to say 'good-bye' to my family with no known return date. After we said goodnight to the girls on the night of my departure, I sat and cried over the ache of missing out on their next few months of growth. I grieved for any loss that they may feel in my absence. Taka said nothing, but held me as I cried.

So it was, that I arrived in Dallas, Texas. My parents picked me up and we drove the last leg of the journey to Houston, TX. As we entered the outskirts of Houston, I called the hospital to ask them about my appointments. This was on Friday, February 28th. I had not yet had any confirmation of an appointment but had gone on faith that it would be there. As we got closer to the hospital, I received a call with a list of all the appointments I was scheduled for over three days the following week... How blessed to receive such confirmation! My uncle also fielded another blessing by offering up points for us to stay at a hotel for free while we awaited appointments, tests, and results.

After all the initial tests, scans, and images, we had a clearer diagnosis of the severity of Masato's condition: He had a grade 3 Chiari II Malformation in which the spinal column was completely blocked by the cerebellum; I was given all the possible outcomes of Masato's abilities, both the worst-case and best-case scenarios. I met the whole surgical team and discussed the details of the planned surgery and its risks. I met with the geneticist, neurologist, urologist, orthopedist, anesthetist...a whole lot of "-ists". They patiently took me through every step and answered all my questions with care.

One other blessing came. As I said before, there was an unspoken stigma about the possibility that Masato's diagnoses were the cause of some congenital defect owing to the fact that there were several of my blood relations who had some or all of the same issues. God's grace poured forth from the geneticist who, though only having my DNA to compare to Masato's turned to me in our meeting and said, "Is there anything else that we can say to assure you that this is not your fault?" She pointed out how his chromosomes were all in order with only a minor addition to one, and one that had no known affect attached to it in any other scientific research. This affirmation that I was not the cause of our son's diagnoses brought a soothing balm to my worst fears.

Another side note about the surgery: I was also strongly advised to not have any other children because of the nature of this surgery. They would open me hip bone to hip bone, pull out the womb and make an incision to expose Masato's back, close his spinal cord, close his back and then put everything back inside and close me up. With a wound on the womb like this, there is an increased risk of rupture and imminent death in subsequent pregnancies. This is also the main reason that any mother undergoing this type of surgery is ordered to bedrest for the duration of her pregnancy.

At the end of all these meetings, the head doctor for my case told me to take a few days to consider before making a final decision. I informed him that I did not need such time since Taka and I had already prayed about it and would do whatever it took for our son. Having heard that, I was put on the surgical schedule for March 11th, when Masato was 25 weeks and 4 days (all inutero surgeries of this kind cannot take place beyond 26 weeks).

The two Sundays prior to the surgery, my parents and I had attended a church in the area. Another blessing came from another area in that of giving us the name of a Church that had a place called Faith House 2 that ministers to people undergoing hospital treatments and was well within the 7-mile radius that we were recommended to stay within in case of emergencies. My mom contacted them, and we were accepted to stay following the surgery before I would be cleared to travel back to Missouri.

On the morning of the surgery, a couple from the church we had visited came to the hospital to sit with my parents while Masato and I were in surgery. They prayed and listened until they were told that we were out of surgery. The surgery was deemed a success. In fact, prior to the surgery, Masato's feet remained fairly flaccid. But a post-surgery ultrasound showed him cocking his feet for the first time. This was a clear and visible answer that the surgery had worked in his favor and gave us hope that he would be able to walk someday.

By the 15th we were in a hotel, again provided by my uncle for the first two nights after being discharged. Mom and I then moved to Faith House 2 while Dad returned to Missouri to take care of some of his commitments.

Over the course of the next couple of weeks, we were blessed with visitors from the church in Houston, friends traveling through from Missouri and even our Pastor and daughter from our sending church in Canada. I felt truly blessed. By March 28th, I was cleared to make the road trip back to Missouri. We broke our trip into four phases with stopovers with family in Montgomery, and with friends in Dallas and again in Oklahoma. While in Oklahoma, we attended church with our "second family" and I was blessed with the laying on of hands and prayers over Masato and me. This is when I found out that on the way driving down to pick me up in Dallas in February, that church had done a surrogate prayer of healing for me through the representation of my parents. God's mercies never cease to amaze me.

Meanwhile, back in Cambodia, Taka was having his own share of stress. A youth team had arrived to stay at Gateway and this particular visit instituted even more change and regulations for future teams coming to Gateway. Having a younger generation afoot proved to be a very strange animal indeed. The use of smart phones was nearly constant, which meant that there was little inter-action with the children aside from showing them the cool things on their phones. Even when Taka took them out for a treat hoping for conversation, he was dismayed to see that no one initiated inter-action without their phones in hand. The crucial point is to ensure that all who enter Gateway must follow the rules of Gateway.

About the time the team was leaving Gateway, my parents and I arrived back in Missouri that first week of April and I settled into the routine of being on bedrest. My parents were able to borrow a wheelchair from their church so that I could join in on outings without exerting myself unnecessarily.

With my parents 40th anniversary coming up in mid-May, they had already planned and booked a trip to Hawaii. God provided me with many women in my parents' church who would come and stay with me during the mornings and afternoons and my best friend came out to either stay overnight with me or to take me back to her house for the night. She also took me to my appointments. Having this community around me helped me to connect with the people in my parent's church. This allowed me a closer connection of the heart, other than the brief encounters I had had the previous years when I would visit their church only a few Sundays.

Taka was also experiencing the blessing of community in the form of two different women from Japan who came at different times during my absence to be with Taka and help ease some of the burden of caring for all of our Gateway kids and keeping a close eye on Lin and Senoka. These two women allowed for Taka and the girls to take a couple of short staycations in the city. It was just further affirmation of God's grace and mercy on us, especially with the added stress of having some Gateway kids leave Gateway-one under favorable circumstances, the other due to disciplinary issues.

Back in the states, my parents had returned and I gave birth through cesarean at exactly 37 weeks on May 30th. The most blessed thing was to see how Masato screamed and kicked!! Kicking was a tremendous blessing after hearing all the worst-case scenarios of the possible use of his legs! He weighed 5lbs, 6oz, which meant that he was allowed to stay in my room instead of being put in the NICU, another answered prayer.

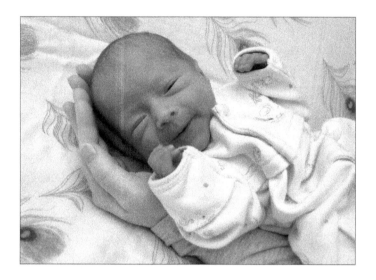

The next question to be answered was whether or not Masato would need a VP Shunt[15] to further help his hydrocephalus. His initial brain ultrasounds showed that his hydrocephalus was stable: neither increasing nor decreasing. I was hopeful that once I had my 6-week clearance from my surgery that we would be able to plan to head back overseas by mid-July. However, when Masato was about six weeks old, his neurologist was concerned with Masato's hydrocephalus and recommended inserting a shunt. Knowing the potential risks, I opted to return to Houston for a second opinion.

---

[15] Healthline, "What is a Ventriculoperitoneal Shunt?" https://www.healthline. com/health/ventriculo peritoneal-shunt , accessed August 20, 2019.

I was devastated by the delay in returning to my family. I had put much hope in returning as soon as possible, and now I would have an indefinite wait.

So, my parents drove with me back down to Texas and made an appointment with the same neurologist who did his spinal repair in March. The doctor there assured us that though the ventricles were enlarged, that there was no need to put in a shunt at this time. His doctor also gave the green light for travelling and I booked tickets to Japan to spend a week with Taka's parents and family before traveling with them to Cambodia.

All throughout the time that I had been in the states, I had an on-going mental battle about all the negative comments people were saying about Masato. It seemed that many people couldn't get past the name of his diagnosis and predetermined that he would be handicapped, not only physically, but mentally as well. Even in the years that followed, people have said things to recant their initial suspicions that he would be "slow" in development. I am able to stand back and praise God for the miracle that he is, and he is a healthy boy with limitless abilities before him.

By the time we arrived in Cambodia, we had been gone just two days shy of 6 months. What a sweet reunion it was. Taka's parents stayed with us about a week before returning to Japan.

Chapter 15

Returning Home and Moving Forward

*O*ver the next three years (2015-2018), we were stretched with a steep learning curve in more ways than one. Aspects in our home life included homeschooling Lin and Senoka while balancing care for Masato and keeping on top of his needs. In our ministry, it was a juggling act to keep tabs on our kids, to move with the shift in the direction of the government regarding care centers, the sale of our property, and navigating the ever-changing dynamics of our life here in Cambodia.

I started homeschooling using Sonlight in 2011. While I loved the plethora of books that came with each curriculum, by 4th grade we came to the conclusion that it was no longer a good fit for Lin's particular temperament. After fielding suggestions and seeking advice of the homeschooling moms whom I knew, I took a leap and changed to Abeka in the middle of her 4th grade school year. Senoka finished off her 1st grade with Sonlight before switching to Abeka in 2017.

Among my daily teaching, I continually researched what medical care is available in Cambodia for Masato. However, for the most part, most doctors were not trained in pediatrics, which need a specialized training not available in Cambodia. I cast a net for information of pediatric specialists in the country but found none. Such a devastating realization—to think of all the children being born with disorders, and when parents are unable to seek care in the neighboring countries, the children suffer and/or die young. This was when I also first started noticing how big a veil is up shielding and hiding all kinds of handicapped and disabled persons here in Cambodia.

In light of this, I do not hide Masato. I answer questions as openly as possible. There is still much to be learned about medical conditions among the general populace and some statements and questions can be hurtful if I let them. However, I know that most statements about how pitiful Masato is, etc, are made in ignorance and they don't get to behold the wonder that he is.

In the spring of 2017, we approached a lawyer to help us seek legal guardianship of Lin. It took some time and effort to compile the dossier needed to approach the courts, but in the end, I was granted sole legal guardianship of Lin (apparently there is a law that allows only one person this status over a Khmer national). With this new status, we are now able to travel with Lin without having to go through the lengthy 1-month process of applying for a permit to travel with her. The whole process took nearly nine months to get to the point where we appeared before the judge.

The summer of 2017, I made the very daring choice to travel with all three kids to the States. Taka, took on the role "papa bear" and requested trackers for the girls to have on their persons. This was also the last trip we took with Lin where we had to request the travel permit. That same summer, my brother and his family moved to Missouri, having arrived about a week before we did and we were able to reconnect after years of living apart. In fact, the first 3 or 4 weeks of our stay was cramped because we were all staying at my parents'. Through this bit of chaos, it was a blessed time to meet and get to know them a bit better.

In September of 2017, Senoka was diagnosed with an inguinal hernia and Taka accompanied her to Bangkok for a repair surgery. It turned out that she had a mild inguinal hernia on the opposite side, and both were repaired at the same time. This meant that she had to drop out of ballet while she recovered. Initially she was very upset about this, but a blessing came later that the performance that was to take place in November had to be postponed to the spring, which meant that Senoka was able to join her classmates after all.

As for Masato, the year 2015 brought two more surgeries: a decompression in Bangkok to help alleviate his Chiari II Malformation.[16] Admittedly, this was the hardest surgery I beheld. I was in Bangkok alone and when they administered the anesthesia, I watched as all color drained from his face and he stopped breathing. The nurses instructed me to lay him on the operating table and to go back to the room while they took care of my son. I was so shocked by what I saw and so overwhelmed with fear over Masato's condition! And there I was, without Taka or someone to hold my hand and pray with me. But God knew and He sent someone. About thirty minutes after I returned to the hospital room where I was to wait, I was blessed with the company of another missionary from Missouri living in Thailand. She stayed with me and prayed and encouraged me until after Masato was brought to the PICU for recovery. We ended up staying in the hospital 4 days and then at my cousin's house another week before being cleared to return home to Cambodia.

When the follow-up a couple of months later revealed that though there was some positive outcome, it was deemed necessary to pursue other treatments to help alleviate his mild hydrocephalus. It was at this point that I reached out to St Louis Children's Hospital in Missouri. When we were accepted as new patients,

---

[16] Mayfield Brain & Spine,"Chiari Decompression Surgery" https://mayfield-clinic.com/pe-chiari-surgery.htm , accessed August 21, 2019.

I made one-way reservations for the two of us and we flew to Missouri, again unsure of how long our stay would end up being. After going through a whole day's appointments to cover all the specialists necessary for ongoing care for spina bifida patients, the neurologist recommended doing a newer procedure to give Masato an internal shunt that, if successful, could mean that he will never need an external shunt. It was there that his third surgery was done: a procedure known as ETV/CPC.[17] The result of which was enough to ensure that he would not need an external shunt.

This was also the time that Masato was diagnosed with a neurogenic bladder that was causing a grade 4 kidney reflux on the left side. Treatment included oral medication and clean intermittent catheterization to empty his bladder every 3-4 hours.[18] We also added cone enemas to keep his bowel movements regular. Another addition to Masato's wardrobe was the assistance of AFOs (Ankle-Foot-Orthotics).[19] It was with these that he was able to start to learn how to use his legs to walk. Eventually, we purchased him a reverse walker and, in March of 2018, his first set of forearm crutches. I had found a trained pediatric physiotherapist in Phnom Penh and I began taking him to a monthly assessment and to receive new exercises to continue his progress for building muscles and balance for ambulation. However, when this therapist and her successor left Cambodia, his home therapy has been done solely by

---

[17] Boston Children's Hospital, "ETV/CPC Procedure", http://www.childrenshospital.org/conditions-and-treatments/treatments/etv-cpc-procedure , accessed August 21, 2019.

[18] Healthy Children.org, "Clean Intermittent-Catheterization" https://www.healthychildren.org/English/ health-issues/conditions/chronic/Pages/Clean-Intermittent-Catheterization.aspx , accessed August 21, 2019.

[19] The Royal Children's Hospital Melbourne, "Ankle-Foot Orthoses, AFOs", https://www.rch.org.au/ orthotic/info_for_parents/anklefoot_orthoses_afos/ , accessed August 21, 2019.

me following the exercises and recommendations I was left with before their departures.

As for our ministry, we were faced with many changes in this season. For one thing, the shift in the Government's focus of care centers, as well as the status of foreigners living and working in the country on business visas threatened our ability to remain in the same capacity as we had been up to that point. It was then that we decided to pursue a change in the status of our ministry and work in Cambodia. Essentially, we came out from under the umbrella of the local NGO and, by God's grace, were able to establish ourselves as an international NGO as of October 2017. During this process, we had to make some changes to our home to meet the prerequisites for the new regulations. These included the addition of 3 more bedrooms as well as renting a separate apartment for our boys to live since the new regulations did not allow for care homes to be co-ed.

For our Gateway kids, we had a solid core of children living with us and did not add any new kids from 2013 until the beginning of 2019. In this time, we experienced great spiritual growth, especially among our older children. In fact, in September of 2017, we held a baptism ceremony at the beach where 14 Gateway kids, along with Lin and Senoka, were baptized. Taka and I have gone through periods of different approaches to discipleship among the youth and children at Gateway. Some initiatives have been short-lived and others for only a season. In spite of our human flaws and inconsistently, we stand amazed at the work God is doing in the hearts of all our children.

The girls involved with the dance studio flourished in their gifts and talents there. They were given more opportunities from the ministry of the studio for their development, including learning how to teach movement and dance to smaller children, mentoring younger dancers and choreographing dances. This did put an added strain on Taka since he was ferrying kids back and forth to the studio up to 7 days a week at one point. In 2017, we purchased 2 motorcycle scooters and this relieved Taka of most of these chauffeuring duties.

Out of this partnership with the studio, our girl with the ballet scholarship had taken the Royal Academy of Dance (RAD) Foundations I exam in Bangkok in June 2018. For her efforts, she was awarded "distinction" and, coming out of this, she was then faced with a huge decision regarding the continuation of her formation as a dancer and an artist. As an 18-year-old, this was a crucial age for increasing her craft; however, it was also the beginning of her senior year in High School. In Cambodia, the toll on the senior students is very great indeed and students spend nearly 70 hours a week in the classroom and doing schoolwork. It was not conducive to hours of studio work on top of this. And so it was, after fielding her prospects: 1) stay in school and enrolling in only 1 dance class a week and put her dance formation and development on hold for the next year; or 2) drop out of school and focus full-time on her dance, she opted for the latter after much prayer.

Our oldest boy was able to pursue his varied interests in the realm of fine arts with a short course at a community college and, later, graphic arts (to a degree) when his friend introduced him to computer animation. We helped him get a Wacom device that allows him to "draw" on the computer. He took to this new device and while corroborating with another Gateway youth, he wrote and illustrated a short children's book, all on the computer.

2018 also saw our first ever High School graduate. Incidentally, she was also the first to finish High School in her whole family. In the months that followed her graduation, she worked to submit an application to be considered to study in America through an organization called She-CAN[20]. This presented another learning curve in helping her refine her English skills through tutoring and also having her attend a well-known school for English nearby. However, after passing the first two hurdles, she was not selected to continue. With this no longer an immediate option, we encouraged her to find a university to attend to reach for her goals.

---

[20] She-CAN, https://www.shecan.global/ , accessed August 21, 2019.

In the summers, some of the older kids have started getting jobs or apprenticeships for their own development and experiences; including, car mechanic, waitressing, and reception positions. At one point, 6 of our girls were volunteering for an international pre-school. In 2018, a new technical training school came and did a soft-skills assessment of our children and, seeing as we were a Christian NGO, (and with our permission) bridged the gap with how each individual has their own specific gifts from God for His purposes.

This particular session with our youth spurred me on to start holding weekly Bible studies among the youth, splitting them into three groups: the oldest girls (grades 10-12), the boys (grades 7-11), and the middle girls (grades 8-9). Our first study was to understand our own individual temperaments and how we are called within our unique designs. After my annual trip to the states with Masato, I brought home and took them through a 6-book discipleship study that traversed from beginning faith to how we live and grow in faith and ultimately take it to the nations.

There was still the matter of our initial property in the province. In late 2015, we were connected with a couple desiring to work in ministry in Cambodia and had been told about our vacant property. After meeting with them, we entered into a lease-to-own agreement with them, but after two years of struggling with this arrangement and after several revisions of the contract, we mutually dissolved the contract and sold the property outright to another person. By the time this was finalized in 2018, we were simply relieved to have it off our hands and no longer had to have it hanging over our heads.

Another aspect to our life at Gateway was that of receiving and housing volunteers for varying lengths of time. Early in the life of Gateway, Taka and I decided that we would be open to accept any volunteers, believer or not. This was in large part due to Taka's own unique experience of being a non-Christian working with a Christian NGO. It was through his experience with the team he worked with that God opened his heart to accept Jesus. In the same way, we knew that short-term work is mostly about the development of the individual, not primarily about what they bring to the project they are joining. Though we do not force volunteers to join our Sunday home services or other Bible Studies, most of the time, they do join. Our prayer is that God's truth will reverberate in their hearts and bring them that much closer to Christ.

There have been some regular visitors to our home over the years. One such individual comes for the specific purpose to serve our family to allow us a short staycation in a nearby hotel. She has been coming since 2014 and we are always so blessed with her heart to help us have these moments as a family a couple of times every year. Then, in 2018, she went beyond what we had ever dared to hope in arranging for a team to come visit, along with two other partners, and stay at Gateway to allow our whole Miyano family to travel together out of the country. It was the first time we had ever left the country with all five of us. We traveled to Japan and spent a week with Taka's family. It truly was a huge blessing.

"God leaves us here because he has a mission for us to fulfill. We aren't here by accident; neither are we here simply to enjoy the good things life has to offer. We are here because GOD put us here, and HE has a sovereign purpose in keeping us here."

–Billy Graham[21]

---

[21] Quoted in *The Hole in Our Gospel* by Richard Stearns, Thomas Nelson, 2014.

Chapter 16

And So We Continue

*N*ow it is the year 2019. Some changes are happening in Gateway. First of all, we have received 5 new children, the youngest of which is 7 (according to her birth certificate).[22] It has been a huge adjustment having to revert to our early struggles with helping the new ones integrate into a home with rules and regulations; along with them, expectations on their obedience and consequences for disobedience. We continue to ask the older Gateway kids to help come alongside the new ones to mentor them and help them to understand this new lifestyle. We have integrated them into the chore groups and they are delegated their tasks accordingly.

However, though the newest three have been living at Gateway for three months (as of August), the new process for accepting children through the proper channels keeps getting more intricate and complicated. The frustrating thing is that, when the new changes were surfacing, everyone we talked to each step of the way merely pointed out where we had skipped steps or made mistakes, until

---

[22] In Cambodia, it is not common practice to request a birth certificate after giving birth. Usually, the parents wait until the child is big enough to start attending school, which usually means that they can't be certain of the exact date of the birth of the child and make assumptions based on what season it was, etc.

finally we had an official walk Taka through the whole process for reintegrating one of our children to the community.

Before this, though, we experienced the rather unfortunate and discouraging event of having one of our girls decide that she no longer wanted to live here. We had been keeping an eye on her and struggling with her rebellious behavior for the last three years. In March, her rebellions came to a head and we gave her an ultimatum while advising her how her decision will affect the rest of her life. However, no matter how much we talked with her and asked her to change her attitude and behavior, it fell on deaf ears. We contacted her grandparents (jobless and living in a shack on someone else's property) and Taka took her to their commune to bring the matter to the officials. Sadly, this girl of 15, not yet finished with 9th grade, had decided her path of hardship. The last news from her was that she had applied to work at a nearby factory.

Following this departure, we have had to deal with some ripple effects that it has had on other children who are in our care. One such girl began acting out and openly stating that she wanted to leave Gateway. When pressed for a reason for her decision, she could only point to the way that her reasons were like that of the other girl who had left. When I had her talk to her aunt, she was told that there was no way that she would have a place to live with her or any other relations owing to, not only their poor living conditions, but also out of a desire to see her flourish with more opportunities that she would have while living at Gateway. Her behavior has improved somewhat, but we can never be sure just how much stock we can put in this turnaround.

Every time we have a disciplinary problem of this magnitude, we know that this will possibly open a doorway for others to plunge into as an easy means of escape. We know that there are some in our care that are merely here out of necessity and that they have "no choice" (like the girl mentioned above). This is not our desire for any who would live here. We want all to aspire to something greater than themselves – to strive for something worth living for. Yet, culturally, when things are difficult, the common thing to do is to simply run away. And, point in fact, in July yet another child departed Gateway because he did not see the point or the reasons behind our parameters and rules. He even went so far as to skip school in the days leading up to this decision. It is a frustrating dilemma that we have been faced with time and again – when we can see the potential in the child staying and the contrast of what a life "outside" could mean – a life of struggle, a life of potentially continual poverty.

This latest experience opened a venue of understanding with the local department and we were finally given a more concrete understanding of the process for receiving and reintegrating children. The ultimate decision comes from the department of the Ministry of Social Affairs and all the processes go through them. We are simply there to present our availability for receiving and/or our conditions for reintegrating children. The ministry is the one to assess the current and future living conditions in view of what is in the best interest of the child. This is something that is potentially good, but we know that there will always be some special circumstances and we will have to weather those cases as they come.

As for our ballet dancer, she and the dance studio team began working with her toward developing and strengthening her abilities and her craft as a dancer and an artist. She had different kinds of classes nearly every day of the week, while she also assisted in the younger dance classes. As they looked to her future, they understood that her formation as a dancer could not be completed much beyond her current abilities were she to remain in Cambodia. So began the search of other dance schools and programs in other countries.

After much prayer and consideration, they helped her make a video audition and she submitted it to the world-renown school called Rambert School of Ballet and Contemporary Dance in London. Her acceptance is miraculous in our human eyes, being one of 20+ applicants accepted out of hundreds who applied worldwide. As an international student, she does not qualify for government financial assistance, so we began praying and the studio team began working tirelessly to raise funds to send her. As a testimony to God's provision, an anonymous donor provided above and beyond what is needed for this first year of study. Also, through the dance and the homeschool co-op communities here in Cambodia, connections were made and she has secured housing with a Christian family for her first year. All of these, along with her visa being issued in record time without follow-up documentation requested nor an interview required, allowed us to send her off to London more than four weeks before her classes begin on September 9, 2019.

Life continues to move forward for everyone at Gateway. We cannot mark our number of children as a meter for success or failure. Yes, it is discouraging when children leave Gateway with only a short-sighted sense of freedom. We have been entrusted with these children. We can only strive to not only teach, but to lead by example. We are not perfect, but we can continue to pursue a God who is. God gave us a vision early on in our lives here in Cambodia. This last year, I attended a retreat conference called Journey Deeper and it was through these retreats that I was reminded once again of the burning desire God had ignited in my heart even before we knew any one of our Gateway children. Even before we would suffer the loss of children choosing to leave Gateway. Through the workshops of the retreats, I was blessed with the tremendous vision that God gave to us for our life here in Gateway and how I fulfill my part in the work and lives of those we serve and raise:

**In keeping Jesus first and allowing Him to use
me, it is my passion and greatest desire to work**

together with my spouse in teaching, equipping and discipling <u>all</u> who are entrusted to our care, giving them solid Biblical training and continue to hold them with open hands to God – knowing that they are ultimately His, in hopes that He and His Spirit will work in their lives to be spiritual leaders surrendered to Christ, realizing their gifts and empowerment by the Spirit to do His work in their homes and in their community – being ambassadors for Christ, leading the way to break the bonds of spiritual, emotional and mental poverty as they themselves discover who God made them to be and partnering with Him on the glorious journey to fulfill His purpose for His own glory and to pass the torch to those who follow until this nation is set ablaze for Christ and Satan no longer has any claim or foothold.

I look back at all that God has seen us through and I can only stand in awe. Only He could have orchestrated this symphony. Only He could have woven the intricate fibers that make up our life here in Cambodia. For no other reason would we be here. Many times our human/fleshly hearts wanted to give up and move on. But God would inevitably show us His hand, His promise, His faithfulness to assure us that we were, and are indeed, on the path He has laid before us.

Our lives have been designed for a time such as this. We continue one step at a time, trusting that God will continue to lead and confirm and affirm us. We pray that God will pull us back when we venture astray from His purpose or His plan. God has placed people in our lives to challenge us and to encourage us and we continue searching His Word and seeking His will through prayer. Not all who enter Gateway will remain there. Each must choose his or her own path. Our task is to teach truth and Christ who is Truth. It is their choice to follow and to what extent. We pray for each precious individual who comes into our care – no matter how brief a time, hoping that the links in their chains of faith will only bring them closer to a relationship with Him. This is our prayer for our Miyano children as well. As parents, we are to provide and protect and, most importantly, to project the Truth of who God is and who they are in Christ.

We will still struggle. We will still falter. But we have a God who is faithful. We have many standing with us all over the world as they pray with us and for us and for each of our children and for our continued faith. And though we cannot claim to know the future of each of our children, Miyano or Gateway, we continue to entrust all to His care as we strive to be good stewards of their care and upbringing.

CPSIA information can be obtained
at www.ICGtesting.com
Printed in the USA
FFHW012315011019
55347468-61080FF